More Psalms for all seasons

by
DAVID ALLAN HUBBARD

William B. Eerdmans Publishing Company
Grand Rapids, Michigan

Library of Congress Cataloging in Publication Data

Hubbard, David Allan.
  More psalms for all seasons.

  1. Bible. O. T. Psalms — Meditations. I. Title.
BS1430.4.H8   242   74-32469
ISBN 0-8028-1596-0

The Scripture quotations are from the Revised Standard
Version Bible and are used by permission.

Contents

Introduction

How do we account for the sustained popularity of the Psalms? Why is it that a collection of prayers, hymns, and teachings nearly three thousand years old still attracts millions of readers every year? Is there an adequate explanation for the fact that guitar-strumming teen-agers use the Psalms for their lyrics, while cane-carrying grandparents refresh their spirits with verses memorized in childhood?

It is not just quaint curiosity — this persistent use of the Psalms. The Psalter is not just an antique shop in which people browse to find a cute thought to place on a shelf or hang on a wall.

It is not just academic interest — this continued preoccupation with the Psalms. The one hundred-fifty poems are not just an archeological mound in which scholars dig to find out how an ancient people lived and worshiped.

It is not just aesthetic intrigue — this perennial perusal of the Psalms. Israel's prayer-book is not just a museum or gallery where men and women admire the artistic enterprise of bygone generations.

No, the reasons for the age-long durability of the Psalms lie much deeper. Men and women for a hundred generations have found in the psalmists of the Bible kindred spirits — kindred spirits whose aspirations and frustrations, whose hopes and doubts, whose blessings and sufferings ring true with our own. The Psalms are not just their hymns and prayers; they are ours.

Who can count the factors that make these songs attractive to us? Literature so beautiful, so perceptive, so devout, so expressive has a hundred different ways of insinuating itself into the consciousness of its readers.

But I think I speak for more than myself when I mention three such factors. First, Israel's singers showed a *readiness to face the facts of their existence.* They lived in no fantasy world; they escaped to no fairyland. They lived in a land that knew drought, plague, famine, and invasion as a steady diet. Idolatry, immorality, and witchcraft fought an endless battle against their covenant faith. They took all that life hurled at them as a people and as persons, and they trusted their Lord in the midst of those circumstances. Even more, they took full measure of their own sinfulness and cast themselves on God's mercy to help them deal with it.

A second factor that makes us moderns eager for kinship with the psalmists is their *intimacy of relationship with God.* His covenant with them was as much a part of their reality as their suffering. They knew the Lord was their God and they were his people. And they acted on that knowledge. In celebration, they blessed his name. In despair, they begged his help. What they felt toward God they expressed. Their trust in him set them free to be themselves before him. They wasted no energy on religious games; they expended no effort on masking their feelings. With a freedom born of confidence in his love, they gave full vent to their anxieties, their expectations, and their praise.

One other lesson we long to learn from these poets of faith: they demonstrated an *ability to apply their faith to their circumstances*. The compartments into which we are tempted to divide life they rejected. Wholeness was their aim. Believing in God's lordship over all their living, they tried to read both prosperity and disaster in terms of God's will. In times of blessing they knew to whom to turn. Their relationship to God was not just a phase of life; it was life's heart.

Credit for editing and typing these chapters goes to my wife, Ruth. Only those who have seen the rough scripts from which I originally broadcast these talks on "The Joyful Sound" can appreciate her contributions. Marion Matweyiw, of our office staff at Fuller Seminary, also helped with the typing. The cordial welcome accorded the earlier volume of meditations on the Psalms makes us dare to hope that this little book will be used to demonstrate afresh the remarkable power, the refreshing relevance, the spiritual honesty of the biblical Psalms.

CHAPTER 1

What to Do
When the Going Gets Tight

Psalm 4

It was our first night aboard ship. Ruth and I were sailing to Liverpool on the way to begin my graduate studies at St. Andrews University in Scotland. We settled in our cabin, an inside stateroom with no porthole. In the middle of the night I woke up with a start and found myself in the deepest darkness I had ever known. The pitch black of the cabin plus the cramped shelf of the lower bunk that I was lying on conspired to make me feel hemmed in. I panicked, dressed quickly, and scurried to the upper deck. To be sure I felt foolish, but at the moment my emotions were stronger than my reason. It was the fourth day at sea before I managed to stay in that tight, dark cabin all night long. And then we left the door ajar to let in some light.

Claustrophobia, we call this. Fear of being hemmed in, shut up in a tight place. Like all phobias, it is a distressing, unnerving experience. And when people contribute to our feeling of crampedness, it is even worse. Have you ever climbed a narrow, winding stairway in a tall church tower or a monument, like the Statue of Liberty? If people are dragging their heels ahead of you and stepping on your heels behind, you can find the ordeal threatening, even nerve-wracking. You have the feeling that if you had to get out in a hurry you'd be trapped,

11

perhaps trampled, by the crowd. Everything within you cries out for room.

Pushy people can make us feel hemmed in even when we are not on a narrow stairway or a tight passageway. If people disagree with us about things that are important, like our religion, and push their disagreements, we feel crowded. If people question the validity of what we believe and drive their questions home, we feel crowded. If people challenge our values and priorities and bore in on us with their challenges, we feel crowded.

"Back off!" we want to shout. "Get off my back! Give me room!" Something like this must have been the experience of the psalmist who wrote the fourth psalm. He had known that cramped feeling that comes from being pushed by aggressive people, and he looked to God for help. "Answer me when I call, O God of my right! Thou hast given me room when I was in distress. Be gracious to me, and hear my prayer" (v. 1).

"Room . . . in distress" is how he describes his greatest need at that moment, and from his experience we can learn what to do when the going gets tight. We are always amazed at how much of ourselves and our situations we see in the Psalms. They are "Psalms for All Seasons" because they touch the whole range of human living with accuracy, honesty, and devotion.

Face Your Problem
Were we to sit down and chat with the psalmist who gave us Psalm 4, we could undoubtedly gain advice. We might say to him, "Sir, you were obviously in deep trouble, trouble of mind and spirit, when you prayed to God your prayer that he was pleased to preserve in the Holy Scriptures. Your problems

12

seemed pressing, yet your confidence in God re-mained strong. You seemed to come through the difficulty with your faith and devotion unscathed. How did you do it? What advice can you give me?"

"Well," the psalmist might reply, "the first thing you must do is face your problem. In my case, people were actually mocking my faith, claiming that it did no good to trust God in a time of drought. The crops were threatened; the livelihood of the land was in jeopardy. And I insisted that we must continue to pray to God for help. He alone could send the good rain we needed. It was this rain that people were praying for in the short prayer that I quoted in the psalm: 'There are many who say, O that we might see some good!' (v. 6).

"This good that they wanted to see was actually rain. When it did not come in time, they were frus-trated. Many were tempted to look to a pagan god like Baal, the Canaanite fertility god. When I in-sisted that the Lord of the creation and exodus, the God of Abraham and Moses, was the only One who could help, they turned on me with bitter and harsh attacks.

"And I had to face my problem and take it to God. If I had tried to avoid it, it would not have gone away. It might have grown even more painful, and besides, if I run from my problems, how do I bring them to God for help?

"One more thing I feel about this," the psalmist might continue. "Facing my problems openly helps me not to magnify them. When I keep them in, they build up inside me to larger-than-life propor-tions. They loom so large that I begin to doubt that anyone can help me with them, even God. That's why, when I pray, I tell God exactly how I feel and then ask for his help."

13

Trust the Lord

At this point we might interrupt the psalmist's flow of conversation and say something like this: "Part of what I hear you saying is that you trust God at the same time that you face these problems. Now those enemies of yours were crowding you, pushing you to turn your back on God and join them in their pagan rites. They were mocking your faith in God, because you held steady in your trust, and still no rain had come. What kept you firm? Why didn't your faith flag?"

"Two reasons, I suppose," the psalmist who gave us this fourth psalm might reply in this imaginary conversation. "First, I remember the past acts of God. I have been in these tight situations before. In fact, I was bold enough to remind God of this in the beginning of my prayer: 'Thou hast given me room when I was in distress' (v. 1). I knew I could bank on God, because he has never let me down. Not that he has always done everything I wanted just when I wanted it. Sometimes the waiting has been painful. But God has always seen me through.

"That's been his pattern in the history of our people. He promised Abraham a son, and then made him wait a long time, testing and strengthening his faith. But in the end he kept his word and honored Abraham's confidence in him. When our people were in Egypt they wondered whether God had abandoned them to the ruthless masters who used them as slave laborers. But God had Moses in mind, and in due season he took us out of enemy territory and gave us a homeland. Why was I able to trust God when he was silent and my enemies were not? Because I knew what he had done for me and my people in the past.

14

"But along with that I also knew something of God's purpose for his people in the present. I tried to put this across to my attackers when I confronted them face to face: 'But know that the Lord has set apart the godly for himself. The Lord hears when I call to him' (v. 3).

"Fellowship with God, that's what life is all about. Those who know God are set apart for him as a wife is set apart for her husband. She has special claim on his time and energy, and he has special concern and regard for her. God will take care of the godly because he is working out his purpose through them. He has called them to worship him, to keep his commandments, to share his love, to make his name known across the land. I knew I could trust God even when the going was tight, because he had special duties for me to carry out and he was going to protect me while I did them. If harm were to come, that too would be part of God's purpose so I could still trust, whatever the circumstances."

Care About Your Opposition

"Before you go on," we interrupt, "let us ask about something you said. You mentioned a confrontation with your enemies in which you told them certain things about your relationship with God. Why did you bother to talk to them at all? They were dead set against you."

The psalmist might pause a minute here to collect his thoughts, and then slowly begin to put words to them. "As God's special people, we have unusual obligations toward our enemies. Four hundred years of slavery taught us what it means to be an oppressed, despised, hated people. When God finally rescued us, he told us to bend over backward to keep from treating people the way we had been

15

treated. Care about your opposition. They too are people, made and loved by God. This is part of my advice along with my previous pointers: face your problem and trust the Lord.

"Caring for those who are against us does not always mean that we are attracted to them. What it does mean is that their welfare is a major concern along with our own. In fact we may have to be stern with those who oppose us, as I was in that fourth psalm that you've been asking about. For instance, I had to challenge the disrespect in which my enemies held me. 'O man, how long shall my honor suffer shame?' (v. 2).

"All that I stood for as a man of Israel and of faith was under assault. My beliefs, my integrity, my reputation were being tarred. I had no choice but to let my accusers know that they were wrong to damage the standing of a fellow citizen.

"But even more strongly I had to question their idolatry: 'How long will you love vain words, and seek after lies?' (v. 2).

"I put the question to them straight. More than *my* honor was at stake. By worshiping idols they were telling lies about God, defiling his name, shaming his honor, perverting his character. I had to try to help them see what they were doing. Enemies they may have been, but I had to care about them as people, whose final destiny was in jeopardy.

"Then I tried to rebuke their temper. Their hostility toward me and others of true faith had heated to the fever point. They could only hurt themselves and others if they kept on smoldering in resentment against us. My words to them were direct: 'Be angry, but sin not; commune with your own hearts on your beds, and be silent' (v. 4).

"Finally, I wanted to encourage them to true worship: 'Offer right sacrifices, and put your trust in the Lord' (v. 5).

"In the long run, if I was to be a faithful representative of God's people, I had to be more concerned for his worship than for my welfare. It was just here that my enemies went astray. When the going got tight for them they had nowhere to go but to their silly idols. And how long can we take aid and comfort from voiceless objects of wood and stone? If they had truly worshiped God, neither my enemies nor I would have been in trouble. I had to tell them that."

"That's an amazing story," we tell the psalmist. "But how did it come out? What happened to you as you faced your problems, trusted the Lord, and cared about your opponents?"

"That's the best part." He smiled as he answered. "It can be put in two words — joy and peace. I had more joy in the drought than most people have at harvest (v. 7). And I had peace to spare. With God's good care I never had a sleepless night" (v. 8). This is where the psalmist's conversation ended and our lesson begins.

Prayer: *Give us, our Father, the psalmist's perspective. Teach us to look into ourselves and face our problems, to look up to you and strengthen our trust, and to look at others, even our enemies, and care about them. We have heard, Father, how one man did it. Now help us to do the same when the going gets tight. In Jesus' name. Amen.*

CHAPTER 2

How to Deal
with Our Enemies

Psalm 5

Bad people we find terribly disturbing. Just hearing about them puts us on edge. With ambivalence we read the reports of crime in the city. With a combination of disgust and fascination we watch the TV bulletins flash the pictures and criminal records of wanted men.

Our attitudes are mixed as we watch the wickedness around us. A fear of being hurt, a desire to retaliate, a temptation to imitate — at different times and in various situations these attitudes churn within us. We find them hard to handle.

Take the hijacking episodes that are almost a weekly occurrence somewhere in the world. We who have to travel a lot, or who have loved ones who do, find that nervousness comes easy. We walk through electronic testing devices and past the peering of U.S. marshals. Even then, on the plane, we watch warily for any ominous packages or bizarre behavior. Bad men, bent on doing wickedness, have made us fearful.

The headline spoke of cattle-rustling. I could scarcely believe my eyes, so I talked with some of my Canadian friends near Calgary, Alberta; they confirmed the reports. Then they gave me a further shock. "There is talk of forming vigilante groups to shoot or lynch the rustlers," they added. The impact of evil — what a terrible thing it is. Bad men force us to bad reactions. Their greed pushes us to be vindictive, vengeful. Their lawlessness lures us to take the law into our own hands. Bad men, bent on doing wickedness, can make us hateful.

And they can do something even worse. They can tempt us to imitate their evil ways. Have you ever seen a play or read a book whose hero was an attractive crook? Did you find yourself identifying with him, hoping that the long arm of the law would not quite reach him? At such times we are tempted to believe that crime *does* pay. After all, there are people who live outside the law with great success, basking in their prosperity, proud of their achievement. Such bad men, bent on wickedness, may tempt us to compromise our convictions.

We do not like any of these attitudes — not the fear of being hurt, not the desire to retaliate, not the temptation to imitate. Bad men there will be, and deal with them we must. As long as wickedness persists (and nothing suggests that it's going out of style), we have to be ready to handle it as carefully, as maturely as possible.

The psalmists of the Old Testament were experts in doing this. They often found themselves surrounded by men who resented their faith, who mocked their beliefs, who belittled their concern for right. Dangerous men, spiteful men, hypocritical men, deceitful men — the psalmists knew them all. And they kept their faith strong in the midst of such company. Their prayers can serve as a model for our response.

Psalm 5 is a good example. The psalmist has been slandered by wicked men, men who use their tongues like poisoned darts to wound and maim him. What their lies were we do not know. They may have accused him of a crime he did not commit, or they may have spread through the community vicious rumors questioning his integrity or his family's: "For there is no truth in their mouth; their heart is destruction, their throat is an open sepulchre, they flatter with their tongue" (v. 9).

More important to us than the psalmist's specific problem is his devout response. His predicament becomes an occasion for worship. His relationship to God is recorded convincingly. From his experiences come four words of advice, advice that applies to anybody facing people who seek his harm: commit their case to God; read them for what they are; refuse to go their way; rejoice in the lot of God's friends. These four bits of advice are as timely now as they were in that distant day when a man, troubled by enemies to his cause, went to God in prayer. Psalm 5 is in every way a psalm for all seasons.

Commit Their Case to God

The psalmist knows where true help lies. "Give ear to my words, O Lord; give heed to my groaning. Hearken to the sound of my cry, my King and my God, for to thee do I pray. O Lord, in the morning thou dost hear my voice; in the morning I prepare a sacrifice for thee, and watch" (vv. 1-3).

The prayer rings with urgency. God is the only one who can help. As king, ruler, judge of all life, it is up to him to do what is right to the man who is being persecuted. Early in the morning this man has gone to the Temple and sacrificed to God to make clear both the urgency of his plight and the fervor of his commitment.

Neither fear of his enemies nor vindictiveness toward them can take hold in his life because he has committed their case to God. He knows that God is more concerned for righteousness than he is, and he praises God for this concern. "For thou art not a God who delights in wickedness; evil may not sojourn with thee. The boastful may not stand before thy eyes; thou hatest all evildoers. Thou destroyest those who speak lies; the Lord abhors bloodthirsty and deceitful men" (vv. 4-6).

His dependence is on God, not as a grim and chancy last resort, but as the powerful, righteous Judge of all the earth who always does what's right. To him the psalmist eagerly commits his enemies' case.

Read Them for What They Are

Seeing how God views wickedness helps us to read our enemies for what they are. Our fallen nature has a certain affinity for evil people. We find them attractive; we secretly wish that we could do what they do and get away with it.

Knowing how God feels about wickedness brings us out of such fantasies. The reality of their depravity comes into view. Boastful, bloodthirsty, deceitful men are not to be imitated but to be pitied and deplored.

Our local newspaper fell into a bad habit for a while. The man who wrote the headlines was continually placing humorous captions above the stories of crime and violence. I'm sure he meant no harm with his joking about criminal deeds and his punning on the plight of innocent victims. But his whole treatment of bad situations lacked seriousness. Finally, I wrote a letter to the managing editor. He got my point, and the paper changed its policy.

Bad behavior is attractive enough to our rebellious spirits. It does not need to be decorated with

21

humor. "Read them for what they are" is part of the psalmist's advice to us when we are tempted to fall in step with evil people. If God, who cannot be corrupted, does not delight in wickedness nor let evil sojourn with him (v. 4), then neither should we.

Refuse to Go Their Way

One of the highlights of this psalm is the contrast the poet draws between his trust in God and the rebellion of his enemies. Bloodthirsty and deceitful are apt labels for his enemies. Their speech is vain flattery at best and hurtful lying at worst. Their eyes are so closed to God's ways that they do not expect judgment. But judgment is all they are going to get.

In contrast, the psalmist describes his own devotion, not in a proud, self-righteous tone, but in grateful appreciation to the Lord whose name he loves: "But I through the abundance of thy steadfast love will enter thy house, I will worship toward thy holy temple in the fear of thee. Lead me, O Lord, in thy righteousness because of my enemies; make thy way straight before me" (vv. 7-8).

This man of faith has refused to go the way of his enemies. Not his own cunning but God's mercy has become his hope. The great reality that steadies and sustains him is "the abundance of thy steadfast love." Refusing to take God lightly as the rebels have done, he realizes that all of life depends on God's grace.

God's house has become his home. He worships God in awe and reverence. And through this worship, he learns where he fits, who he is, to whom he belongs. Resisting all temptation to insolence, he gladly humbles himself before his God and recalls God's goodness to him.

God's way has become his path. To God he looks for direction and protection. Like a veteran guide God leads the man who trusts him through foreign and hostile terrain. With God at his side, he fears neither the attacks of his foes nor the danger of getting lost.

The godless know none of this hope and security. Their ways lead to self-destruction: "Make them bear their guilt, O God; let them fall by their own counsels; because of their many transgressions cast them out, for they have rebelled against thee" (v. 10).

"Refuse to go their way" is the psalmist's good counsel. "God has infinitely better plans for you."

Rejoice in the Lot of God's Friends

These better plans he sums up beautifully in the closing verses: "But let all who take refuge in thee rejoice, let them ever sing for joy; and do thou defend them, that those who love thy name may exult in thee. For thou dost bless the righteous, O Lord; thou dost cover him with favor as with a shield" (vv. 11-12).

Rejoice in the lot of God's friends, the psalmist urges. Joy and blessing are what a loving God sends to them.

This is a remarkable ending to a psalm that began with groaning. In the beginning the psalmist lamented the attacks of God's enemies; in the end he celebrates the destiny of God's friends: joy and blessing.

The end result of trusting God even when bad people seem to have the upper hand is not just passive acceptance of a tough situation but vital joy in a good God. Not the blows of wicked enemies but the blessings of a God who covers us "with favor as a shield" is the poet's last word.

When opposition heats up, when ungodly people seem to be gaining ground, when wickedness looks like a winner, the psalmist's advice will come in handy — not advice based on hollow theory but advice founded on the rock of his own experience. Don't be afraid of being hurt, he says. Squelch your desire to retaliate. Refuse to compromise or imitate. Leave their cause with God; read them for what they are and refuse to go their way. Then rejoice in the lot of God's friends. His final word to them is joy and blessing. And that's a word worth waiting for.

Prayer: *Father, you helped our psalmist in a difficult situation. Evil is just as powerful today as it was then. But so are you. Jesus Christ tells us that you will help us in temptation as you helped him. Teach us to take his word for it. In his good name. Amen.*

CHAPTER 3

What to Do
When God Seems Far Off

Psalm 10

Tom was obviously edgy as he came into my office. He sat down with a heaving sigh, held his head in his hands for a moment, then shakily began to speak. "I-I've lost God," he blurted out and waited anxiously for my answer.

Though Tom's experience may have been more dramatic than most, we all know something of what he felt. We have all been through times when God seemed far off, removed, absent, beyond our reach.

The spiritual nature of our faith aggravates this. At times it seems that we have no one tangible to touch, no audible voice to listen to, no visible being to fix our gaze on. We grope and stumble reaching out to a God who does not seem to be there. We raise our voices to the heavens with passionate requests for God to answer, and our words bounce off the ceiling and ricochet around the walls.

Tom and I talked about this, God's silence, his remoteness. Tom was not alone in feeling that he had lost God. Nor was his sensation something new. The Bible, that book of God which brings him near to his people, knows plenty about this feeling that God is far off. Some good men have felt this way on occasion.

The nameless man of faith who gave us Psalm 10 was one of them. He watched wicked men work their evil schemes and go unscathed. He heard their blasphemous boasts, their arrogant outcries, and wondered why God did not come on the scene and settle with them. At stake were the justice of God and the welfare of his people. Yet God's response was only silence. But the psalmist did not quit. His trust was too strong and his concern too great. From his prayer my friend Tom, and a lot of others like him, can learn some splendid lessons. After nearly three thousand years this experience of this psalmist is still practical and profitable. Psalm 10 is a psalm for all seasons.

Tell God How You Feel

Our psalmist's courage is commendable. He minces no words in telling God how he feels: "Why dost thou stand afar off, O Lord? Why dost thou hide thyself in times of trouble?" (v. 1).

God's absence is almost never felt when things are going well. Seas are smooth, the sky is bright, and we just assume that God is on hand taking care of his own. But let the tensions build and the frustrations mount, let life put its knee in your middle and start to pin you to the mat, and all of a sudden God seems to be gone.

When this happens, do what the psalmist did. Tell God how you feel. This will help because it will remind you that God is near enough to hear your complaints. God's program is not like a poorly managed restaurant. You know the kind — the food is cold and tasteless and the service is poor. A frustrating combination this is, because when you try to complain to the waiter about the wretched food you can't even get his attention. Your vexation grows because your discontent mounts with every bite, yet you don't even have the satisfaction of making your distress known to the management.

The God of the psalmist is not like that. Though God may not be doing all that the psalmist wants when he wants it, he is within reach of the psalmist's prayer. The psalmist knows this and raises his complaint to God.

And he doesn't spare the details. What he feels he says. Thoroughly, forcefully he describes his problem in all its ramifications. In verse after verse the psalmist reminds God of what his enemies are doing. Then earnestly, passionately he calls on God to act: "Arise, O Lord; lift up thy hand; forget not the afflicted" (v. 12).

By telling God what he feels he both unburdens his own spirit and expresses his trust in God. The psalmists were not silent sufferers. They took their complaints directly to headquarters, especially when they thought that headquarters was partly responsible for their complaints.

Remember God's Lofty Ways

The core of the psalmist's complaint was that wicked men around him were committing all kinds of mayhem and getting away with it. God not only seemed far off to the man of faith but also to the cynics and skeptics of the community. In fact, they went so far as to pay no attention to God. No morning found them in the Temple offering morning sacrifices. No evening found them recounting his glories to their families by the fireside. "In the pride of his countenance the wicked does not seek him; all his thoughts are, 'There is no God.' His ways prosper at all times; thy judgments are on high, out of his sight; as for all his foes, he puffs at them. He thinks in his heart, 'I shall not be moved; throughout all generations I shall not meet adversity' " (vv. 4-6).

Talk about misinterpretation, the wicked man has completely misread God's remoteness. He has pushed God out of the picture entirely. In fact he has made himself god, beyond any word of criticism, above any form of judgment. Self-sufficient, self-satisfied.

Into this appalling account of arrogance, our good poet tucks an important phrase. We don't want to miss it. "Thy judgments are on high, out of his sight" (v. 5).

This one clause, like a mighty wrecking crew, tumbles the wicked man's entire world view. It collapses like rubble around his head. He believed that because he could not see or feel God's judgment, there was no God around to judge him. The psalmist knows better. God was making his judgments all right, but he was keeping them on high, out of the sight of the brazen rebel.

In the Graduate School of Psychology at Fuller Theological Seminary we have a program to help shy boys. These youngsters, eight or nine years old, play in a special room under the leadership of one of the students. Through a microphone and ear plug receiver the psychologist gives instructions to the leader that the other boys cannot hear. The psychologist and some of the mothers watch the boys at play through a one-way window. They see the boys clearly through the glass but the boys are not at all aware of them. They evaluate the boys' behavior and reward them as they break away from the shy patterns and enter into play with one another. Without knowing it the boys are being judged by one who sees them but whom they cannot see.

So it is with God and his dealings with men. His judgments are out of man's sight. But he knows full well what we do and why we do it. "Remember God's lofty ways" is another good word of advice that we get from this psalm. Just because we do not see God does not mean that he is absent from our scene.

Avoid the Mistakes of the Godless

Our psalmist spends a lot of time describing the harsh deeds and bitter attitudes of the wicked. His primary reason for doing this is to support his argument with God. He thinks that God should judge them swiftly and surely, and God has not done so. In great detail he gives evidence of their crimes and pleads for justice: "In arrogance the wicked hotly pursue the poor; let them be caught in the schemes which they have devised" (v. 2).

His accusations become even sterner as he pictures the wicked as a wild animal crouched to ravage his prey: "He sits in ambush in the villages; in hiding places he murders the innocent. His eyes stealthily watch for the hapless, he lurks in secret like a lion in his covert; he lurks that he may seize the poor, he seizes the poor when he draws him into his net" (vv. 8-9).

This is wickedness compounded. Arrogance is bad enough. But here it is coupled with cruelty, cruelty in its worst form — oppression of the poor and defenseless who have no one to stand up for them.

In these descriptions the psalmist is piling up evidence before God, arguing hard that God should judge. But beyond that, he is urging his hearers to avoid the mistakes of the godless. They are to be pitied and censured but not to be imitated. Their example is a terrible warning of the depths to which the human spirit can sink if it misinterprets the silence of God. "Why does the wicked renounce God, and say in his heart, 'Thou wilt not call to account'?" (v. 13).

Foolishly they seize on God's silence as the opportunity to shatter his laws. A colossal mistake, a tragic one that we should avoid at all costs.

Let the Experience Strengthen Your Faith

Our psalmist knows better. He trusts God's constancy despite his silence. God's character is changeless; he knows that. What he is he is, whether man sees that or not. For a time he may seem to pull back, and it looks to us as if our circumstances are out of hand, totally awry. But God does not change. His love remains firm; his sense of justice stays keen. "Thou dost see; yea, thou dost note trouble and vexation, that thou mayest take it into thy hands; the hapless commits himself to thee; thou hast been the helper of the fatherless" (v. 14).

Picking on the poor and oppressed, on widow and orphan, is an especially risky business, because God has special concern for them. This reminder of God's care strengthened the faith of the psalmist.

And so did his recognition of the thoroughness of God's judgment: "Break thou the arm of the wicked and evildoer; seek out his wickedness till thou find none" (v. 15).

Ultimately silence would give way to action. Remoteness would become involvement. This had ever been God's pattern, and the psalmist was willing to put strong trust in God's constancy. "The Lord is king for ever and ever; the nations shall perish from his land. O Lord, thou wilt hear the desire of the meek; thou wilt strengthen their heart, thou wilt incline thy ear to do justice to the fatherless and the oppressed, so that man who is of the earth may strike terror no more" (vv. 16-18).

Honest with God, mindful of his lofty ways, shunning the mistakes of the godless, strengthened in faith by his experience, the psalmist learned and taught what to do when God seems far off. He knew what my friend Tom had to learn. When we feel that we have lost God, we must remember that God has not lost us. He knows right where we are and just what we need.

Prayer: *Father, we ask not so much that you will draw nearer to us as that we will draw nearer to you. Keep us so near to you that even your silences will speak to us. Don't let us miss any lesson we need to learn, whether lessons of joy when you seem near or lessons of trust when you seem far away. Through Jesus Christ, who is the only way to you, we pray. Amen.*

CHAPTER 4

What to Do
When You Are Tempted to Drop Out
Psalm 11

Even your best friends can be wrong. They mean
well. They have tried to assess your problems with
care. They struggle to share your agony and to
suggest a sound solution. But they can be wrong.

It takes a lot of wisdom to weigh their advice
and decide whether or not to follow it. And it takes
a lot of courage to go against their counsel, when
with all good will they have offered it.

This was the situation in which our psalmist
found himself. His friends were urging a course
of action that they were sure was best for him. They
had only his good in mind. They had tried to read
the circumstances accurately. But they were wrong,
and the psalmist had to tell them so.

That's where the psalm begins: "In the Lord I
take refuge; how can you say to me, 'Flee like a bird
to the mountains . . .'?" (v. 1). The friends had used
their best judgment. They measured the pressures
that were pushing in on the psalmist, and they
measured his ability to take those pressures. When
they had completed their calculations, they had a
simple word of advice for the man in trouble:
"Head for the hills. What dove continues to sip
the water when the small boys are throwing pebbles
in the pond? What raven keeps on pecking at the
grain once the farmer aims the slingshot his way?

Birds may not be smart, but they know enough to get out of the way when the stones begin to fly. You should do the same." So goes the counsel of the friends.

They had some good evidence on which to base their counsel: " 'for lo, the wicked bend the bow, they have fitted their arrow to the string, to shoot in the dark at the upright in heart' " (v. 2). *The enemies were formidable.* Like archers hiding under cover to ambush their prey, they waited for the psalmist with murder in their eye. Their wickedness had made them ruthless; their superior weapons gave them confidence; their secure hiding place strengthened their nerve. The odds were overwhelmingly against the psalmist. He must run.

The cause was hopeless. So the friends judged the psalmist's situation: " 'if the foundations are destroyed, what can the righteous do?' " (v. 3). The political, social, and spiritual life of the land was crumbling. The foundations of truth, justice, and piety were being undermined by a flood of wickedness. No one righteous finger in the dike could stem those tides.

As usual, the psalmist was frugal with his words. He gave us little clue as to who these enemies were or what they were doing. In all probability, they were men and women who had rejected Israel's traditions. They despised the covenant and its standards of righteousness. They rejected the worship of the one true God. And they busied themselves making life difficult for anyone who was serious about the faith. Apparently they did this with considerable success. To the psalmist's friends they seemed to be winning. Why else would they advise him to run?

It seems likely that the psalmist was a leader. He may have been a king like David, harassed by his own son Absalom. He may have been a prophet like Jeremiah, persecuted by kings and princes.

Whoever he was, you can be sure that the pressures were great enough to tempt him to drop out. No doubt there were moments when the words of his friends seemed to make sense. At times he may have been on the verge of packing his bags and heading for the mountains, where the rugged terrain and the hidden caves offered shield from the arrows of his enemies.

Many of you know how he felt. You live in homes where your faith is made fun of. You have husbands or wives who despise the ways of Christ. You are tempted to drop out. And your friends may encourage you to do just that. This psalm is for you. Let the psalmist who knows how you feel become your counselor.

Some of you work in places where your Christian witness puts people on the spot. Your sense of fairness makes them uncomfortable. Your attitudes and values clash with their practices. They demand compromises that you are unwilling to make. You are tempted to drop out. This psalm is for you. Let the psalmist who has sat where you now sit become your teacher.

His answer to the friends who urged him to "flee like a bird to the mountains" came in four parts. It was based on his view of God. He did not dispute his friends' evaluation of the evildoers. The situation was every bit as bad as they said. But he saw more than they. From his wider — and higher — perspective, he had the good sense to reject their counsel and offer some of his own, counsel that pointed to a new relationship with God: believe

34

in the presence of God; trust in the righteousness of God; count on the power of God; rejoice in the fellowship of God. Let's see how this fourfold suggestion sheds light on the psalmist's predicament — and on ours.

Believe in the Presence of God

"The Lord is in his holy temple, the Lord's throne is in heaven" (v. 4). These words are the key to the psalmist's faith. He is no naive optimist. He mouths no glib platitudes about silver linings behind the clouds. The problems are real, but so is the presence of God. In the Temple his words can be heard, his power can be recounted, his glory can be seen.

The saving God is present. Believe in him. The God who overturned the might of Pharaoh is among us. The God who toppled Jericho's tall walls is in our midst. The God of Gideon and David has dealt with enemies before.

"Flee to the mountains," the friends had whispered. "Your enemies are beyond your handling." "Go to the temple," the psalmist sang, "and know that God is greater than the enemies."

No God of a local shrine is he, no provincial deity. He is the high God, Lord over all. Earth cannot contain his throne; it stretches through the vast reaches of the heavens. Everything and everyone on earth — friend and foe alike — must reckon with his presence.

Trust in the Righteousness of God

"If the foundations are destroyed, what can the righteous do?" (v. 3). That was the desperate question of the friends. The psalmist's answer helped to lift the dark despair: trust in the righteousness of God.

"His eyes behold, his eyelids test, the children of men. The Lord tests the righteous and the wicked, and his soul hates him that loves violence" (vv. 4-5). The psalmist would not want us to misunderstand what he means by the righteousness of God. Especially he would not want us to think of righteousness as a cold, hard list of things that are right and wrong. He would see God's righteousness as God's commitment *to do what is right in all situations.* More than anything else, doing what is right means *to do what a relationship requires.* God's relationship to the wicked requires judgment; his relationship with the righteous requires blessing.

Just here our poet would want us to understand something else — what he means by the wicked and the righteous. These, too, are words of relationship. The wicked are those who care nothing about their relationship with God. The righteous are those for whom their covenant with God is the center of their living. Wickedness and righteousness are as much matters of commitment as of conduct, as much matters of attitude as of action, as much matters of devotion as of deeds.

As God scrutinizes men and women with those piercing, testing eyes, as he pointedly peers into the quality of our lives with eyelids lowered as though to help his focus, he is testing our loyalty more than our acts. Are we for him or against him? That is the essential question. Wicked people may do some good things, and righteous people may do some bad things. It is not sinfulness or sinlessness that is at stake. It is basic allegiance, ultimate loyalty.

The psalmist knew to whom he belonged; he was not at all ambivalent about his loyalty. That's why he could trust God's righteousness. He knew that God would do what his righteousness required — he would save the psalmist at the time and in the way he deemed best: "For the Lord is righteous, he loves righteous deeds" (v. 7). Our righteous deeds? Our acts of loyalty to God? Of course he loves them. But more important, he loves to do righteous deeds for us. Not our righteous deeds but God's righteous deeds are the theme of this song. God loves to deliver, to rescue, to save, to redeem those who look to him. That's an unbeatable assurance when we are tempted to drop out.

Count on the Power of God

If the righteous have this kind of assurance, the wicked have quite a different kind: "On the wicked he will rain coals of fire and brimstone; a scorching wind shall be the portion of their cup" (v. 6). Part of what the psalmist learned in the Temple was the terrible judgment that would befall those who did not pledge allegiance to the one true God. Their fate would recall the terrible destruction of Sodom and Gomorrah. Doubtless, our poet friend had often heard that story recounted in the Temple. The rescue of Lot was an illustration of God's care for his own. The burning, searing devastation of Sodom and Gomorrah was an illustration of the terrors of judgment. In his mind's eye, he had stood with Abraham and looked down at the desolation that forever erased the cities of the plain: "and [Abraham] looked down toward Sodom and Gomorrah and toward all the land of the valley, and beheld, and lo, the smoke of the land went up like the smoke of a furnace" (Genesis 19:28).

Flee like a bird to the mountains? Not the psalmist — he counted on the power of God. Not he, but his enemies, should do the fleeing.

Rejoice in the Fellowship of God

The final word is in some ways the psalmist's best: "the upright shall behold his [God's] face" (v. 7). What really keeps us from dropping out as the pressures mount? The joy of fellowship with God. What often keeps the seamen alive who bob day after day in a rubber dinghy on treacherous seas? The thought of seeing the faces of their loved ones. What frequently helps prisoners of war survive torture and stave off suicide? The hope of gazing again on the faces of their families.

Letters can be a great help. They bring words of comfort and cheer. Phone calls are even better. The sound of a voice helps to sharpen the memory of a face. (I write this in the airport at Utica, New York, refreshed by a few minutes of chatting with my wife on the phone.) But face to face, that's where real fellowship is.

The face, more than any other part of the anatomy, expresses the person. To behold the face of God is to be in direct touch with his magnificent love; it is to be personally acquainted with his majestic holiness; it is to know firsthand his unqualified acceptance.

Flee to the mountains? Not at all. Cling to God's fellowship. Rejoice in the delights of his companionship. Look lovingly upon his face. In that look you will find strength and hope and healing.

Tempted to drop out? Of course! We all are at times. And sometimes we do take refuge in the mountains temporarily to gain strength and perspective to return to the pressures of the valley.

But at other times we cannot flee. Even when our friends urge us to, we cannot flee. But we can endure the opposition, the enmity, the ridicule of those who are threatened and annoyed by our faith.

We can endure if we see more than our enemies do, more even than our friends. We can endure if we see God present with us, rescuing us in his righteousness, judging in his power those who oppose him, and calling his own to constant fellowship. Our look at him, and especially his look at us, are more than enough to keep us from dropping out.

Prayer: *Lord, help us to know that you really are Lord – present, powerful, concerned. Let the reality of your lordship loom larger than any pressures we face. Through Jesus Christ, we pray. Amen.*

CHAPTER 5

What to Do
When the World Goes Wrong

Psalm 12

What's wrong with the world? Why is it so fouled up? Why does life seem to fall apart so easily?

In one form or another, questions like these keep pressing us for an answer. They knock on our doors as persistently as a zealous salesman. They telephone as frequently as a teen-aged boyfriend. They call at our windows as stridently as a fifth grade playmate.

What's wrong with the world? How did it get in such a mess? What makes life so painful? Why is it so easy to hurt and be hurt?

The answers to these questions may come in almost as many forms as the questions. But certainly one answer that cannot be overlooked is found in Psalm 12. In his passionate plea for help in a world gone wrong, the psalmist brings us to understand just how the world has gone wrong. More than that, he brings us to understand what God can do about a world gone wrong.

The Basic Problem of the Faithful

"Help, Lord; for there is no longer any that is godly; for the faithful have vanished from among the sons of men" (v. 1). This is a grim analysis. Apparently whole communities were rejecting the ways of God, whole clans were turning their backs on their religious heritage. We may allow for certain overstatement as the bitter fruit of the psalmist's despair. Like Elijah he may have thought he was the only one left among the faithful, when there were still seven thousand who had not bowed the knee to Baal. Yet it is obvious that the outlook was dark: rebellion was rife, and the faithful were few.

It is his description of the rebellion that catches our eye. His cry for help was so pained, his picture of waywardness was so dark, that we brace ourselves to hear the worst about the conduct of these rebels.

Surely they were steeping their lives in idolatry, bowing and scraping to objects of wood and stone. But that's not what the psalmist said.

Well then, they must have been staining themselves in every kind of lust and sexual perversion, abandoning the law of God and the natural orders to destroy themselves in adultery, fornication, and homosexuality. But the psalmist made no mention of this.

Or violence and viciousness must have been their way of life. They must have been oppressing widows and orphans, vandalizing their properties and confiscating their goods. But of these things the psalmist had not a word to say.

Why the call for help? Why the biting complaint about the widespread backsliding? What had gone wrong with our poet's world? Words — that's what. Lying and arrogant words: "Every one utters lies to his neighbor; with flattering lips and a double heart they speak. May the Lord cut off all flattering lips, the tongue that makes great boasts, those who say, 'With our tongue we will prevail, our lips are with us; who is our master?' " (vv. 2-4).

What is so wrong with lying words? To answer this we have to go back to the beginning of human history. When God created man in his image — man

41

who is both male and female — he equipped him with the gift of speech. The first *human* words recorded in the Bible are words that show what words are for. They are words of fellowship: "This at last is bone of my bones and flesh of my flesh; she shall be called Woman, because she was taken out of Man" (Genesis 2:23). Adam's words about Eve remind us that words are for helping, for valuing, for supporting another person. Words are for disclosure. Adam left no doubt, at that moment at least, in Eve's mind. He was open to her; he was for her; he wanted her.

With words he built a bridge from his heart to hers. With words he tore away any veil of mystery and disclosed his mind to her. With words he affirmed her in her womanhood and pledged to her his love.

That's what words are for. And that's why a world full of lying words strikes such terror in the psalmist's soul. Lying is an insult to God, who made us for better things, and to the neighbor, who deserves better of us.

Without truth, fellowship is impossible. There can be no real sharing when deceit crowds out honesty and flattery shoves sincerity to the side.

Lying is a form of violence. It takes a pure relationship and rapes it. It embezzles not a person's wealth, but his reputation. It loots not a man's treasures, but his dignity.

What is so wrong with an arrogant tongue? That question, too, takes us back to the beginning. Man's tongue was part of the equipment God gave him, not only for fellowship with his neighbor but for worship of the one God.

Tongues are made for prayer, not for pride. Their basic purpose is to help us express our dependence, not to declare our self-reliance. The disloyal persons in this psalm viewed the tongue not as an instrument of praise, but as a weapon of attack; not as an altar of devotion, but as a tool for manipulation. Gifted, glib, treacherous — they counted on their tongues to spring them from any trap they might be caught in.

Just words, we say, mere words — not on your life. Words are a badge of our humanity. How we wear them tells how human we really are.

I can't resist inserting an unusual prayer that the United Press International picked up recently. Aimed at politicians, it speaks to us all. It was offered by Harry Moats in the West Virginia House of Delegates: "Make our words gracious and tender," he prayed. "We may have to eat them tomorrow."

The Lord's Own Answer to the Faithful

Our psalmist had pleaded for help. As the men of Israel were accustomed to doing, he had brought his need to God in the Temple. The Lord not only heard his plea, but he also answered it in a more dramatic way than we find in most psalms.

Usually the sufferer laid his requests before God and then accepted by faith the fact that God would answer. Here the answer itself was given. Whether it came in an audible voice we do not know. More likely, God inspired a priest or prophet to share this word of assurance with the man who begged for help. " 'Because the poor are despoiled, because the needy groan, I will now arise,' says the Lord; 'I will place him in the safety for which he longs' " (v. 5). The deceitfulness and the haughtiness of the wicked had gone far enough. Innocent people were being hurt by it. To them, God clearly and personally promised protection.

Exalting the humble and putting down the proud was the way God worked. Now it was time for him to work again. His special compassion for the needy was going to show itself; his peculiar bias toward the poor — especially the poor in spirit who knew they had no help but him — was about to be demonstrated. The God of the slow-tongued Moses, the God of the barren Hannah, the God of the underdog David had spoken. Rescue was in sight.

Words were the problem. We have seen that. But words were also the answer. With lying, arrogant words the world goes wrong. But with saving, rescuing words God protects his people. Evil words are powerful. They cut, maim, bite, sting. But the healing words of God are even more powerful. The psalmist was glad to hear them.

The Final Response of the Faithful

He was glad to hear them, because he knew how reliable they were: "The promises of the Lord are promises that are pure, silver refined in a furnace on the ground, purified seven times" (v. 6). In a *hymn of praise,* the poet sang of God's trustworthiness. When we speak of a silver-tongued orator, we mean he is bright and shining in his persuasiveness. When the man of Israel compared God's promises to silver, he thought of the purity of their truth.

Contaminated, corrupt speech is part of our broken, fallen humanity. We seldom mean what we say or say what we mean. Tarnished, pocked, flecked with dross — our speech looks more like lead than silver. That's why ultimate human hope lies not in *our* word but in *God's.*

From the hymn of praise our spokesman, joined now by some of his friends, returned to his *plea for help:* "Do thou, O Lord, protect us, guard us ever from this generation. On every side the wicked prowl, as vileness is exalted among the sons of men" (vv. 7-8). He returned to this plea not in despair, but in confidence. Not that his circumstances had changed much. The wicked men were still on the prowl, ready to snipe at the righteousness with their vile words. They had not been in the Temple. They had not heard the reassuring words of God. They had not been transformed by the promise that God was for them in the midst of their poverty. But the psalmist had, and his voice rang with assurance as he renewed his plea for God's help.

The power of words — the prisoners of war returned from North Vietnam gave us moving illustrations of it. In solitary confinement or locked in their cages two at a time, they tapped on the thick walls their words of strength and hope. Their code was simple. They divided the alphabet into five rows of five letters each, after pulling out the letter K and adding it as the lone letter in the sixth row. Two taps followed by three taps meant the third letter in the second row. Letter by letter, tap by tap, they sent their signals in defiance of their guards.

The prisoners assigned to sweep the yards outside the cells used their crude reed brooms as transmitters. With swishes instead of taps, they brought daily greetings and news bulletins on prison life to the eager ears cocked in every cell to hear. No one wanted to miss a word. A prisoner who missed the meaning of the swishes would cough so that the sweeper could repeat the code.

Words that brought news, words that kept lonely men in touch with other men, were the lifeblood of the prisons. To some, the words brought eternal life. Passages of Scripture, snatches of hymns, simple prayers were sent from cell to cell to point men to the Word beyond the words, the Word that became flesh and lived among us with words and deeds of truth and grace (John 1:14).

The power of words — they are part of what's wrong with a world where speech can malign, attack, abuse, demean, seduce. But words are also part of the way God gives us strength and hope and courage to live in the midst of the world.

Beyond the words of the world are the words of God, bringing healing in place of hurt, help instead of harm. And beyond the words of God is the Word of God, Jesus Christ the Savior, who alone speaks the message of life.

Prayer: *Father, in the midst of all the speech we hear around us — some foolish, some foul, some fiendish — give us ears to hear your voice. Let it be your words about your Word, and his words about you, that we really listen to. In his great name we pray. Amen.*

CHAPTER 6

How Do I Please God?

Psalm 15

Reuben was out of breath as he raced up the hill. He was glad it was Passover, not Pentecost or the Feast of Tabernacles, that was to be celebrated. Passover came in early spring, and the long trip to Jerusalem was not quite so taxing as it was in late spring and early fall when Pentecost and Tabernacles took place.

But it had been hot enough, especially that last long climb from Jericho up the hill to Jerusalem. For a while during the morning heat, the pace of the pilgrims had slackened. The fatigue of the days of travel began to pile up. The break in the tempo of the walk did not last long once the travelers caught sight of the walls and towers of Jerusalem. In fact, fatigue gave way to song: "On the holy mount stands the city he founded; the Lord loves the gates of Zion more than all the dwelling places of Jacob. Glorious things are spoken of you, O city of God" (Psalm 87:1-3).

As they entered the city their hearts turned specifically to the Temple, the goal of their long journey. With their hearts, their songs turned to the Temple: "How lovely is thy dwelling place, O Lord of hosts! My soul longs, yea, faints for the courts of the Lord; my heart and flesh sing for joy to the living God. . . . For a day in thy courts is better than a thousand elsewhere. I would rather be a door-keeper in the house of my God than dwell in the tents of wickedness" (Psalm 84:1-2, 10).

Reuben sang at the top of his voice as he ran. Singing was not his best skill, but this was a time for enthusiasm, not artistry. So he sang his psalm of longing, longing for the courts of the Lord.

But as the pilgrims began to push their way through the milling throngs at the entry to the Temple courts, their thoughts turned inward and upward. Would the God whose glory filled the Temple accept them? What requirements did he lay upon those who came to worship him?

Warm fellowship, not fine architecture, was their goal. They had not come all that way just to gaze on the beauty of the Temple, magnificent though it was. The beautiful bronze castings and sculpture of Hiram of Tyre glistened in the noonday sun, but Reuben and his friends did not pause to gaze. The two great pillars called Jachin and Boaz, symbols of the might and power of God, towered above them, but they did not crane their necks to peer at them. The massive molten sea with its thousands of gallons of water stood there on the backs of the twelve bronze oxen that faced the four points of the compass, as testimony to the universal sovereignty of God. But Reuben and his companions had no time to admire its splendor.

It was the most high God they were approaching. It was fellowship with him that they sought. If the majesty of the Temple and its trappings caught their eyes it was only to remind them of the greater majesty of God whom no temple could contain.

The Need for Fellowship
At such a moment Reuben and his fellow wor-shipers might have uttered the question with which

our psalm begins: "O Lord, who shall sojourn in thy tent? Who shall dwell on thy holy hill?" (v. 1). For generations, pilgrims had voiced those questions outside the Temple court. It was part of a liturgy that they recited before entering. It brought into sharpest focus the purposes of their coming. Pilgrimage to Jerusalem was more than a holiday outing. It was more than a clan reunion. It was more than a cultural excursion. It was nothing less than encounter with the living God. Reuben thought of this as he chanted the question.

In his spirit he sensed a *deep desire for fellowship with God.* He may even have used, as thousands of worshipers had through the years, the words of another psalm to give shape to this desire: "As a hart longs for flowing streams, so longs my soul for thee, O God. My soul thirsts for God, for the living God. When shall I come and behold the face of God?" (Psalm 42:1-2).

"Think of it, Reuben," he said to himself, "you are to be a guest of God; you are to enjoy his gracious hospitality. That's what it means to sojourn in his tent, to dwell on his holy hill."

Perhaps those closing lines of the shepherd psalm flashed through Reuben's mind as he mused on his desire for fellowship: "Thou preparest a table before me in the presence of my enemies; thou anointest my head with oil, my cup overflows. Surely goodness and mercy shall follow me all the days of my life; and I shall dwell in the house of the Lord forever" (Psalm 23:5-6). God was to be his host — and permanently. That was Reuben's driving desire.

But with the deep desire he also felt *great obstacles to his fellowship with God.* The awesome Temple intimidated him. It reminded him of God's majesty

49

and his own unworthiness. He asked himself: "How can I possibly qualify for fellowship? What right do I have to ask to be God's guest? How dare I seek an invitation into the presence of the Lord of the universe?"

The Terms of Fellowship

Reuben's flow of thought, this flood of hard questions, was interrupted by the chanting of the Temple singers. In their chant, Reuben heard the answer to his question. Who shall sojourn? Who shall dwell? The man and woman committed to God's terms of fellowship.

One by one these terms were spelled out: integrity, honesty, respect for neighbor, concern for God's glory, reliability, freedom from greed. In a few terse sentences the basic human duties were summarized.

Integrity of conduct was mentioned first: "He who walks blamelessly, and does what is right" (v. 2). Reuben, like all Jews who really knew the meaning of their faith, understood life as a pilgrimage, a journey. It had a beginning; it called for direction; it moved toward a destiny. That's why the people of the Bible called life a "walk." Because it was God who determined the path and pace of the walk, the men and women of faith knew that he held them accountable for how they walked. Did they live by his rules or did they not? Did they follow his course or did they not?

Honesty was also a term of fellowship: "and speaks truth from his heart" (v. 2). Deceit was an affront to God. Reuben knew that Israel's God could read the thoughts and motives of his heart. He knew that God desired a close correspondence between the thinking, the doing, and the speaking of his people.

Reuben had often prayed about this in words well known to his countrymen: "Search me, O God, and know my heart! Try me and know my thoughts! And see if there be any wicked way in me, and lead me in the way everlasting!" (Psalm 139:23-24).

Respect for neighbor was something else that God demanded of those who would truly worship him: "who does not slander with his tongue, and does no evil to his friend, nor takes up a reproach against his neighbor" (v. 3). Biblical faith was not manipulation by magic. Reuben thought of this as he heard the Temple singers chant those words. There was not a hint in their song of magic spells, of secret ceremonies, of mystic rites. The surrounding nations specialized in all of this. Their gods had requirements that their worshipers had to reckon with, but how different the requirements were from those of Israel's Lord. Not magical manipulation but social responsibility, neighborly concern, was what God demanded. God, who had created that neighbor, wanted him treated with full respect and dignity. God, who cared for that neighbor, wanted his care demonstrated tangibly in human lives. God, who had lavished his grace upon his people, wanted that grace shared with others.

The neighbor's reputation was to be guarded — no slander. The neighbor's welfare was to be sought — no hurt. The neighbor's mistakes were to be forgiven — no reproach. Reuben's God insisted that our treatment of neighbor was to mirror His treatment of us.

Concern for God's glory was yet another term set by God for those who would have fellowship with him: "in whose eyes a reprobate is despised, but who honors those who fear the Lord" (v. 4). In a fresh way Reuben saw that this made sense, as he stood before the Temple and thought about the meaning of worship. What Reuben was about to do in worship was to cast himself before God, confessing his sins, remembering God's greatness, reaffirming his loyalty to God. Unless he truly believed that God was glorious, all this was stupid. He would not pray to a tree, confess to a rabbit, pledge allegiance to the moon. Because God was great, holy, and loving, Reuben delighted to worship him. What was more right than for this God — this mighty and merciful God — to be worshiped. No wonder a reprobate should be despised — and pitied. He had turned his back on the Lord of all of life; he had treated the King of glory as a worthless trinket. What colossal foolishness, what mammoth stupidity!

Reliability is also required: "who swears to his own hurt and does not change" (v. 4). Here Reuben was reminded of the Ten Commandments. Just as a neighbor's reputation was to be guarded, especially in a court of law where false witness was forbidden, so God's name was not to be treated lightly. A vow was to be kept. An oath taken in God's name, as we take an oath of office or an oath in court, was not to be broken. Devotion to God and love for neighbor demand our reliability. The foolish promise, the empty vow, hurts both.

Freedom from greed is the last term mentioned: "who does not put out his money at interest, and does not take a bribe against the innocent" (v. 5). Financial gain at someone else's expense — this is what God has forbidden. Economic opportunism that capitalizes on another person's problems is inconsistent with true worship. God, who pays special attention to the plight of the poor, the widow, the orphan, the stranger, insists that his people do the same.

How can we worship unless we support the values and priorities of the God we worship? Can we really worship and at the same time say that God is wrong in his requirements and standards? These were the questions that Reuben raised as he searched his heart and prepared to move into the Temple. And he had no doubt about their answers.

Full commitment to God's ways — this is what God required of Reuben, and requires of us. What he requires, he enables us to do. He makes demands and then supplies the grace for us to deal with his demands.

Did you read about Eleanor Stacey? She was all set to graduate from eighth grade in Clifton, Arizona. Her aunt made her a graduation dress, but the principal would not approve it. It had a pattern, and the rules required solid pastel. Eleanor was barred from the graduation. That decision to bar her reverberated across the country and resulted in $300 in gifts, and the promise of a four-year scholarship to college from a man in Missouri. A happy ending to what had to be a miserable decision.

God does not quibble over our dress. He does not ban us from his celebration because we are out of uniform. He has sent Jesus Christ to dress us in his own righteousness. Through him we become part of a glorious Church without spot or wrinkle.

He sets up the terms by which we must please him — total allegiance to his standards and priorities. Then he gives us the grace and strength through Christ to make that total pledge.

Prayer: *Lord, now that we know better who you are, take us as we are and begin to make us what you want us to become. For Jesus' sake. Amen.*

CHAPTER 7

Who Is God but the Lord?

Psalm 18

The further we get from the times and places of the Bible, the harder it is for us to understand what God is saying. The major themes of salvation are clear, of course. People in every era, on every continent, from all types of cultures, have heard the good news the Bible brings and have come to know God's love in Jesus Christ.

But how often we in our twentieth-century civilization miss the nuances that make the Scriptures come to life. Our *urban life* is a barrier to our understanding, for instance. We may have never seen a sower scattering grain by hand, a thresher winnowing wheat and fanning away the chaff, a shepherd edging his flock into a fold, a farmer pruning his vineyard. Yet without these pictures, we miss part of the Bible's message.

Our *climatic conditions* may be an obstacle as well. In cool, green lands watered by melting snows and heavy rains, the premium put on water in the Bible may seem strange. In places where irrigation is no problem it may be hard to grasp the value of morning dew, which the poets and prophets made so much of. Burning sun and scorching winds, which dominate desert life, hold no terror for people who have never been singed or stung by them.

Our *cultural context* often stands in marked contrast to the setting in which God gave the Bible. In places and times where young widows can readily take well-paying jobs to support themselves, and where remarriage is a strong possibility, the Bible's concern for the care and feeding of widows may appear overdone. In an era when overpopulation seems a major threat, when a surplus of workers can bring a sharp rise in unemployment, it is hard to understand why the Bible counts large families a high blessing.

Our *political system* erects a hurdle that has to be surmounted if we are to grasp what the Bible says. Our republics and democracies seem a long way from the monarchies of Saul, David, Solomon, and Hezekiah. Even where kings and queens remain, we treat them more like symbols than rulers. They keep the citizenry in touch with its past; they lend dignity to the ceremonies which promise stability to a changing world; they provide an anchor in the shifting political seas where several parties vie for power. But they lead no armies — our modern kings — they wield little authority, they participate in few decisions of state.

How different were the kings of Israel. In a patriarchal system, the king was like a father to his people. They looked to him for total leadership. When the armies marched, he was usually at their head. When treaties were drawn up, he alone could approve or disapprove. When disputes arose among the tribes over rights to territory or water, he was the chief arbiter. Even in civil suits, like the contest between two prostitutes over the custody of a baby, the king — in this case Solomon — had to make the final decision. The spiritual and moral life of the nation was deeply influenced by the king.

When he took the lead in encouraging true worship, in supporting the Temple and the priesthood, in sponsoring the great festivals, in enforcing the laws of the covenant, the whole nation followed. David, Solomon, Asa, Jehoshaphat, Hezekiah, and Josiah all illustrate this principle. When even good kings like David and Solomon had spiritual lapses, the whole nation drifted into sin and suffering. Like father, like son; like king, like people — so went the pattern in Israel.

Given this central role, it is no wonder that a number of the psalms have to do with the king. *Royal* psalms we call them. They were used on numerous occasions: the coronation (Psalms 2, 72, 110), the royal wedding (45), prayer before battle (20), thanksgiving after battle (18, 21).

Psalm 18 gives us a powerful picture of a king at prayer, a picture of devotion and humility. It shows us royal living at its best, as the king bowed before the unique God, the one and only Lord from whom all true victories come.

A Confidence Based on Experience

The first nineteen verses ring with confidence as the king recounted the dramatic way that God delivered him from deep distress. The experience of rescue that prompted this confidence was so vivid in the king's mind that he thanked God with layer after layer of praise. He built a foundation of adoration with brick after brick of testimony to God's might: "I love thee, O Lord, my strength. The Lord is my rock, and my fortress, and my deliverer, my God, my rock, in whom I take refuge, my shield, and the horn of my salvation, my stronghold" (vv. 1-2). The piling up of terms expresses the forceful superlative: God gave him the strongest protec-

56

tion in his time of trouble. That's what all these terms combine to say — strength, rock (which offers a place to hide), fortress, deliverer, shield, horn (which wards off enemies like the horn of a large animal), stronghold.

To make clear just how powerful this unique God is, the king reviewed *the deep distress* in which he found himself. His language is graphic — "cords of death," "torrents of perdition," "cords of Sheol," "snares of death" (vv. 4-5). There is no way to miss the point. The king and his men were all but doomed. Death had wrapped its strong ropes around them. Strong currents, like flash floods, were sweeping them to their destruction. The grave was not only yawning to receive them, but it had actually snared them in its tough tethers.

The king's desperate cry for help brought *the dramatic intervention* with which God responded. In one of the most moving descriptions of majesty and sovereignty in the whole Bible, the king recounted God's coming, a coming accompanied by a terrifying list of cosmic actions. Earthquakes (v. 7), fire and smoke (v. 8), thick darkness (v. 9), strong wind (v. 10), hail and brimstone (v. 12), thunder and lightning (vv. 13-14), the parting of the waters of the sea (v. 15) — these fierce signs placarded the intervention of God. The universe with all its might cooperated in the rescue. God was on the march, and the whole creation stepped to his cadence.

The poetry is powerful. Its point is not to tell us literally how the victory took place — in fact, a later section of the psalm (vv. 34-45) does this — but to picture for us the all-encompassing power of God. The poetry, with its thundering roar and shining brilliance, gives us flashbacks of other times and other places when God came to his people with victory in mind — the plagues of Egypt, the parting of the Red Sea, the shaking at Sinai, the triumph of Deborah when even the stars in their courses conspired against the enemies of Israel.

The same God, the unique God, was at work. That's what the poetry tells us. The king had learned afresh that there is no God but the Lord. His was a confidence based on experience.

A Relationship Based on Righteousness

Next, the king reflected on the background of his rescue. What gave him courage to call on God? What type of relationship did he enjoy that enabled him to count on God to snatch him from the very clutches of death?

It was a relationship based on covenant loyalty. *The king was totally loyal to God:* "The Lord rewarded me according to my righteousness; according to the cleanness of my hands he recompensed me. For I have kept the ways of the Lord, and have not wickedly departed from my God" (vv. 20-21). No crime of inhumanity ("cleanness of my hands"), no sin of idolatry had marred the king's allegiance to God. He had maintained a right, a true, a loyal commitment. And God honored that.

But much more important was the fact that *God was totally loyal to the king:* "With the loyal thou dost show thyself loyal; with the blameless man thou dost show thyself blameless. . . . This God — his way is perfect; the promise of the Lord proves true; he is a shield for all those who take refuge in him" (vv. 25, 30). To God went the ultimate credit. It was his righteousness — his loyalty to the covenant — that made the ultimate difference. No God but the Lord — the psalmist knew that and rejoiced in a relationship based on righteousness.

58

A Victory Based on God's Enablement

The poem has few parallels in the annals of warfare. In a world where military men compete for rank, honor, and recognition, our king showed no interest in medals or awards. He took no credit for the victory: "For who is God, but the Lord? . . . He trains my hands for war, so that my arms can bend a bow of bronze. . . . For thou didst gird me with strength for the battle; thou didst make my assailants sink under me" (vv. 31, 34, 39). No boasting here, no drumming up of a hero's reception with pushy publicity, no rigging of the record to gain the promotion.

The king knew who supplied the power, who plotted the strategy, who confounded the enemy. No God but the Lord — the psalmist gladly confessed that, as he celebrated a victory based on God's enablement.

A Doxology Based on God's Salvation

Just what victory this psalm commemorated, we cannot know. Probably it was used repeatedly from the time of David on, whenever Israel's armies won the day in battle. The location of the battle and name of the king are not the point of the psalm. The praise of God's salvation is. From beginning to end that is the theme.

The king sang of a *living God*. Let the neighbors of Israel cling to their myths. Let the city-states of Tyre and Sidon, Damascus and Hamath bind themselves to empty idols. Israel's God was alive: "The Lord lives; and blessed be my rock, and exalted be the God of my salvation" (v. 46). The Lord lives! No one who had surveyed the silent battlefield and tallied the damage could doubt it.

The king sang of a *saving God*, "who delivered me from my enemies; yea, thou didst exalt me above my adversaries; thou didst deliver me from men of violence" (v. 48). The Lord saves! No one who had weighed the odds against Israel could give any better explanation.

The king sang of a *loving God:* "Great triumphs he gives to his king, and shows steadfast love to his anointed, to David and his descendants for ever" (v. 50). The Lord loves! No witness to his persistent pattern of rescue for Israel could deny it.

No God but the Lord — how else could the king close his prayer than with a doxology based on God's salvation?

No God but the Lord — Israel's best kings knew that and refused to compete with him. The kings of Egypt, Canaan, and Babylon believed themselves divine. The good kings of Israel knew better and viewed themselves as servants.

No God but the Lord — Israel's true King knew that and came to earth to win victories for us all. In him — God's anointed Son and Servant — the living, saving, loving God showed what real kingship means.

No God but the Lord — we must come to know that and to experience the victory which that knowledge brings. From David's day till now, humble and dependent and grateful prayer is what it means to live like a king.

Prayer: *We thank you, Father, that even governments have a Governor, that even kings have a King. Teach us to live royal lives by bowing daily at your throne in praise and thanksgiving. Through Christ, the King of kings, we pray. Amen.*

CHAPTER 8

How Can We Know About God?

Psalm 19

Have you seen any good sunsets lately? Have you sat by a mountain lake and watched the sun brush the clouds with crimson and then dye the lake with the drippings of its paint? Have you driven along a desert road and seen a sandstone mesa blush when caressed by the soft rays of fading light? Have you strolled along a western beach as the rolling tides turned from blue-green to yellow-gold with the passing of the day?

Have you seen any good sunsets lately? What really did you see as you examined that lovely seam where night was stitched to day? What was on your mind as you approached that boundary that divides the dominion of the sun from the realm ruled by moon and stars? What you saw depends on the perspective from which you looked.

We can look at a sunset from a *scientific perspective*. Of course, if we do, we would not call it a sunset but an "earth-roll." We would know that the sun does not really move; it is the rotation of our twirling planet that makes the sun appear to set. Our technical information would tell us that what we are really watching is an experiment in the physics of light. Light rays (and scientists still don't have all the answers about the nature of light) strike particles of moisture or dust and turn them luminous by reflecting off them. Desert sunsets are the simple mixture of light and dust clouds. Ocean sunsets come from light and water, drops of water bundled together in the packages we call clouds. The scientific perspective makes the whole event seem dully mechanical, but it is one way of looking at a sunset.

The *esthetic perspective* is another. Painters and other persons with keen artistic insight see things in a sunset that most of us miss. They have an eye for color that catches the subtle variations as the sun completes its measured plunge. They have a sense of texture that perceives how the gentle shifting of the clouds sheds its lights and shadows on the sea and changes it from tweed to corduroy to velvet. The esthetic perspective may be beyond the reach of some more matter-of-fact souls, but it is one way of looking at a sunset.

Most of us look at sunsets from an *emotional perspective*. Our emotions may vary as we do. For some, sunsets are a symbol of romance. Couples stand closer and hold each other tighter at sunset. Talk fades to whisper, and touch becomes more gentle at sunset. The sinking light, the lengthening shadows seem to shut out the rest of the world with its worries and struggles, and to lock in the two people with themselves and their love. For others sunset sparks the emotion of loneliness, not romance. The busy activities, the routines of escape, are cut off. Friends and fellow workers have scattered to their homes and the single, solitary person begins to feel that stifling nightly isolation. The cowboy may have sung "I tell you folks, it's heaven to be ridin' down the trail when the desert sun goes down." But there are millions of people watching sunsets who can't agree with him. Their loneliness is too great. Emotions run high at sunset and furnish the perspective for a lot of us.

In analyzing these perspectives that we bring with us at sundown — scientific, esthetic, emotional — we must not neglect the *theological perspective*. "The theology of a sunset?" you ask. "Isn't that taking this business of theology too far? It is well and good to talk about the theology of our relationship to God, or even of our attitudes toward family and government. But sunset? Good grief! That does seem a bit preachy!" Stay with me, and with good help from our psalmist I shall try to show you what I mean.

God Shows His Glory in Creation

"The heavens are telling the glory of God; and the firmament proclaims his handiwork" (v. 1). God's revelation of his power and glory is *cosmic in its scope*. The heavens, the firmament — what we could call the sky — carries the message everywhere. The psalmist chose his words carefully. He wanted to avoid any idea that God's glory could be confined to particular locations or limited to specific situations. The sky is a dominant presence wherever we go on earth. Had the psalmist talked about the glory of God in the sands of Edom or the cedars of Lebanon, he would have been right. He would, however, have left out other climates and regions. But the sky is inescapable. It shrouds the deserts, the mountains, the plains, the seas. If the sky heralds the majesty of God, no one on earth can avoid the message. That is, no one who looks at the sky with a theological perspective.

"Day to day pours forth speech, and night to night declares knowledge" (v. 2). God's revelation of his creative power is *persistent in its rhythm*. There are no pauses in the anthem of revelation. Each day teaches the song afresh to the next day; each night sings the words in the ear of the following night. As the earth is captured under the giant bowl of the sky, so all of time is covered by the calendar of revelation. God, who rested at the beginning, has taken no holiday since. Never has there been a day, never a night, when words of God's majesty, when knowledge of his power, were not passed along to those whose ear was tuned to theological language.

"There is no speech, nor are there words; their voice is not heard; yet their voice goes out through all the earth, and their words to the end of the world" (vv. 3-4). God's revelation of his might and majesty is *eloquent in its silence.* It is inaudible yet articulate. This is one reason why we so often miss the theology of the sunset. Its message of praise and honor to the God of glory is transmitted on a wavelength to which most of our receivers are not tuned.

"In them [the heavens] he has set a tent for the sun, which comes forth like a bridegroom leaving his chamber, and like a strong man runs its course with joy. Its rising is from the end of the heavens, and its circuit to the end of them; and there is nothing hid from its heat" (vv. 4-6). God's revelation of his worth is *all-encompassing in its sweep.* The sun witnesses to it in the zest with which it rises and speeds across the sky, zest like a bridegroom's as he is invigorated with love, zest like an athlete's as he presses toward the tape. The sun witnesses to God's worth as it completes its heavenwide course and leaves nothing untouched by its heat.

But the message of the sun can go unheeded just as the message of the sky or the sunset often has.

The whole pagan world of Israel's neighbors certainly missed these messages. They worshiped the sun and the sky. They were impressed by the scope of the sky, which sent its dark words of thunder and lightning as well as its kind notes of dew and rain. They stood in awe of the sun which brought them light and life, and yet which took its toll in parching drought. The psalmist had one eye on those pagan practices when he taught that a chief purpose of the sky and sun is to shout the praises of the only living God. No gods at all, powerless on their own, their task is to chant His message.

Just here our scientific perspective, drummed into us by our culture whether we are scientists or not, is apt to get in our way. We think of the sun and the sky as objects. We look at them, study them, describe them. Even when we put on our theological glasses — when we try to see them as God's handiwork — we still view them as objects. We say, "What a great God he is to have made that sprawling blue vault; what a great God he is to have set that vast traveling ball of fire in the sky."

This is good. It is better than not seeing God's work in them at all. But our psalm is telling us more. It says that the sky and sun are *subjects* as well as *objects*. We not only observe them; they speak to us. They praise God; they shout his glory, his worth, his might to those prepared to hear. The universe is infused with such vitality by God's creative power that it joins with men and angels in lauding his greatness.

What a God he is, whose universe itself rejoices not only to obey his will but to celebrate his name! That's the deeper message of the psalm. That's a key to the theology of the sunset. It is not just a picture of God's power; it is an actor in the drama of God's glory. It is not just to be watched; it is to be heard. It is speaking to us of God. It is part of the answer to the question, "How can we know about God?"

God Shows His Will in Scripture

Part of the answer, I say, because the psalm says much more about knowing God. In a transition that seems abrupt, our poet begins to speak of the *law* as another source of knowledge. In his poetic style he moves from synonym to synonym to describe the law: testimony, precepts, commandment, fear, ordinances (vv. 7-9). These terms all have to do with God's instruction — instruction transmitted through Moses and the prophets, instruction in what God has done, who he is, and what he requires. This instruction, which the psalmist prescribes with the joy of a doctor who knows our illness can be cured, is found in the Scriptures.

One minute the psalmist has us looking through a telescope at the heavens. The next, he has us peering through a magnifying glass at the Bible. From both places we learn about God.

In fact, the psalmist seems to draw a parallel between the witness of the sun and the voice of Scripture. We can catch a hint of this as we look at his teaching on the *character* of Scripture and the *impact* of Scripture.

The *character of Scripture* is described in terms like these: perfect, sure (dependable), right, pure, clean, true, righteous, desirable (vv. 7-10). In these words are echoes of the brightness, the cleanness, the purity, the dependability of the sun. As its rays do their job bringing life and warmth to men, so does God's spiritual instruction in his Word.

This comparison becomes even plainer in the description of the *impact of Scripture*. It has life-giving power; it revives the soul (the person). It breaks through the dark clouds in our thinking; it makes wise the simple. It lifts the despair that dulls our judgment; it rejoices the heart. It gives bright light for us to see by; it enlightens the eyes. It does not withhold its brilliance; it endures forever. It never lets us down; it is righteous altogether.

What the sun does for our natural lives, the Word does for our spiritual lives. Both speak of God. But the greater eloquence belongs to Scripture. The sky and the sun speak without words. Scripture speaks with the clearest possible words.

In fact, without the words of Scripture, we cannot hear the words of creation. Until we discover how to know God through his writings, we will miss him in his handiwork.

The heavens may tell the glory of God, but to most men and women they do so only in vaguest terms. Like a faintly hummed tune whose words you can't recall, the message of the sky may put you in a mood of wondering about God. But full knowledge of him is gained only as he speaks precisely to us and about us in Scripture. Once he does, and the Holy Spirit helps us understand, we hear his voice in creation in clearest, sharpest words.

Revelation can never leave us untouched. Getting to know God through his Word puts great demands on us. The psalmist found this out.

His knowledge of God called for *contrition:* "Clear thou me from hidden faults" (v. 12). He had learned that there were areas where he needed help even when he didn't know what help he needed.

His knowledge of God called for *loyalty:* "Then I shall be blameless, and innocent of great transgression" (v. 13). He had learned to fear idolatry,

the great transgression, the despicable act of dis-
loyalty to God.

His knowledge of God called for *dedication:* "Let
the words of my mouth and the meditation of my
heart be acceptable in thy sight, O Lord, my rock
and my redeemer" (v. 14).

How can we know God? Our psalmist knew the
answer. By listening to Him speak in creation where
we hear of His power, but especially in Scripture
where He tells us His will.

What the scientific and esthetic and emotional
perspectives cannot give, the theological can. It
alone will clear our eyes to see and open our ears to
hear the greatness and grace of God. Next time you
see a sunset try to *hear* it, too.

Prayer: *Great God of the sunset, great Lord of
Scripture, continue to show us your power and glory.
Great God and Father of Jesus Christ, teach us your
wisdom and your love. Through your Son, your
clearest Word of all, we pray. Amen.*

CHAPTER 9

When Boasting Is Not Bad

Psalm 20

Weary to the point of breaking, the courier had arrived at the palace. In swift, breathy words, like the panting of a dog on a summer day, he gasped out his news to the palace guard and together they rushed inside to alert the king.

The king's face grew dark as the courier poured out his message. He had been dispatched by the base commander at Engedi on the west shore of the Salt Sea. The king's garrison there had been embattled by troops from Moab and Ammon that had skirted the southern tip of the Salt Sea and then moved north against the forces of the king. Judah's borders had been violated; the women and children of her southern reaches were in jeopardy; the crops and flocks of her villages were threatened.

The king's decision was swift. His first move was not to gather his military officers in the army's briefing room; it was to assemble his people in prayer. His nation's first need was not martial strategy; it was spiritual counsel.

It was such a circumstance — an invasion and a call to prayer — that framed the setting for Psalm 20. Though we do not know which invasion prompted it, or which king was actually featured in it, we do have a good illustration of the type of occasion where it would have been used, in the experience of King Jehoshaphat.

This story is told in II Chronicles 20. Here are some excerpts from it: "After this the Moabites and Ammonites . . . came against Jehoshaphat for battle. Some men came and told Jehoshaphat, 'A great multitude is coming against you from Edom, from beyond the sea'. . . . Then Jehoshaphat feared, and set himself to seek the Lord, and proclaimed a fast throughout all Judah. And Judah assembled to seek help from the Lord; from all the cities of Judah they came to seek the Lord.

"And Jehoshaphat stood in the assembly of Judah and Jerusalem, in the house of the Lord . . . and said, 'O Lord, God of our fathers, art thou not God in heaven? Dost thou not rule over all the kingdoms of the nations? In thy hand are power and might, so that none is able to withstand thee. . . . O our God, wilt thou not execute judgment upon them? For we are powerless against this great multitude that is coming against us. We do not know what to do, but our eyes are upon thee" (II Chronicles 20:1-6, 12).

There were psalms for all seasons, including psalms for the eve of battle. How people react in crisis shows something of their inner life. During the sharp Los Angeles earthquake of February 1971, a friend of mine from the east was visiting in Pasadena. As his hotel room began to rock and reel at 6:00 A.M., he instinctively began to pray. Afterward he told me how reassuring it was to him that in the moment of shock his first reaction was to pray, not to curse.

In their better moments the men and women of Israel were like that. Bad news, terrifying surprise, jolting trouble sent them to prayer. And the psalms were their prayer book.

Psalm 20 demonstrates not only the occasion of prayer — the eve of battle — but also the ritual of prayer, a ritual in which priests, lay people, and king all took part.

The priests began the ritual after the king had lifted his petition to God as Jehoshaphat had: "The Lord answer you in the day of trouble! The name of the God of Jacob protect you! May he send you help from the sanctuary, and give you support from Zion! May he remember all your offerings, and regard with favor your burnt sacrifices!" (vv. 1-3).

Next, the people summoned to the Temple in the heat of the crisis expressed their hopes for God's blessing on the king: "May he grant you your heart's desire, and fulfil all your plans! May we shout for joy over your victory, and in the name of our God set up our banners! May the Lord fulfil all your petitions!" (vv. 4-5).

At this point in the dramatic ritual there might have been the hush of silence, the quiet of waiting for the voice of God. Hopefully the Lord would speak to his king and his people through a prophet. This was precisely what happened in Jehoshaphat's case. Here is the chronicler's own description: "Meanwhile all the men of Judah stood before the Lord with their little ones, their wives, and their children. And the Spirit of the Lord came upon Jehaziel . . . a Levite of the sons of Asaph, in the midst of the assembly. And he said, 'Hearken, all Judah and inhabitants of Jerusalem, and King Jehoshaphat: Thus says the Lord to you, "Fear not, and be not dismayed at this great multitude; for the battle is not yours but God's. . . . You will not need to fight in this battle; take your position, stand still,

71

and see the victory of the Lord on your behalf, O Judah and Jerusalem." Fear not, and be not dismayed; tomorrow go out against them, and the Lord will be with you' " (II Chronicles 20:13-17).

It must have been some word like that — some assurance of God's presence and blessing, some promise of victory — that prompted the king in the psalm to utter these confident lines: "Now I know that the Lord will help his anointed; he will answer him from his holy heaven with mighty victories by his right hand. Some boast of chariots, and some of horses; but we boast of the name of the Lord our God. They will collapse and fall; but we shall rise and stand upright" (vv. 6-8).

The liturgy of prayer before battle closed with the priests and people together lifting their voices in a ringing prayer which was also a song of hope: "Give victory to the king, O Lord; answer us when we call" (v. 9).

Why Boasting Is Usually Bad

It is the king's attitude that stands out in this extraordinary psalm. Pride is an occupational hazard with rulers. Their power to command and the allegiance their people pay them tend to make them self-sufficient. They try to deal from strength, and they feel it is important to appear strong no matter what their actual situation may be. Goliath can be counted an example — though a crude one — of the smugness that power often spawns. The book of Samuel records his boasting: "The Philistine said to David, 'Am I a dog, that you come to me with sticks?' And the Philistine cursed David by his gods. The Philistine said to David, 'Come to me, and I will give your flesh to the birds of the air and to the beasts of the field' " (I Samuel 17:43-44).

None of this type of boasting passed the lips of the king in our psalm. His boast was in the name of the Lord. He did not follow the pattern of Jehoash, king of Israel, who once sent this arrogant message to Amaziah, king of Judah, who had wanted to deal with him as an equal: ". . . A thistle on Lebanon sent to a cedar on Lebanon, saying, 'Give your daughter to my son for a wife'; and a wild beast of Lebanon passed by and trampled down the thistle" (II Kings 14:9). A boastful word this little fable was. Judah's king was a mere thistle in comparison with Israel's monarch, who called himself both mighty cedar and wild beast.

Most boasting is bad. It is *an affront to God.* It takes human credit for what are really divine gifts and God-given opportunities. Most boasting is bad because it chokes out worship. It is virtually impossible to sing "Praise God from whom all blessings flow" and "Look what I have accomplished" at the same time.

Most boasting is bad. It is *an insult to persons.* When we give the impression that we are superior, others are tempted to doubt their gifts. We make them feel cheated. Their gratitude to God for what they are may be smothered under the blanket of our haughtiness. And we may also provoke bizarre reactions in others, like defensiveness, where they are taunted into asserting themselves in order to compete with us. In other words, boasting can be catching, like a typhoid epidemic spread by a carrier who does not even know what harm he is inflicting.

How Boasting Is Kept in Check

Psalm 20 prescribes a good antidote to this epidemic of arrogance. It gives a formula for keeping the wrong kind of boasting in check.

God's people gathered in the sanctuary, as the prayer
for the king indicated: "May he send you help from
the sanctuary, and give you support from Zion!"
(v. 2). A declaration of dependence on God — that
is what their gathering meant. They did not mobil-
ize their troops in self-defense, nor flee the city in
panic. They went to the Temple to declare their
hope in God.

Next, *God's people offered sacrifices,* as was their
custom when confronting emergencies: "May he
remember all your offerings, and regard with favor
your burnt sacrifices!" (v. 3). An acknowledgment
of sin and a petition for God's favor — those are
what the sacrifices meant. Neither the people nor
their king paraded through the public squares in
pomp and majesty. They did not rally their horses
nor rattle their sabers. They went to the Temple to
confess their needs to God.

Finally, *God's people honored the name of the Lord,*
as they centered their celebration in him: "May we
shout for joy over your victory, and in the name of
our God set up our banners!" (v. 5). An expression
of adoration — that is what those banners meant.
Not to the regiments was tribute to be paid; not to
the general were the trophies to be awarded. The
Lord's name, the Lord's person, the Lord's glory
was to be the theme of their jubilation.

The boasting was kept in check. God's grace and
power, not human endeavor, became the center of
their living — and especially in the hour of crisis.

When Boasting Becomes Acceptable

When it comes down to it, there are *only two options*
in life. We can boast of the horses and chariots of
our accomplishments — and become obnoxious; or
we can boast of the name of the Lord our God and
become acceptable to him and to others.

"Most of us are spending far too much for defense. Our budget to protect ourselves is far too high." I once began a sermon at a Naval Air Base with those words. You could hear a pin drop. But it was not military expenditures that I had in mind. It was what we spend in kitchen and bedroom, school and office, factory and shop, to defend ourselves.

Either the Lord is our protection or we have none. Our emotional defenses are no match for his righteousness.

When it comes down to it, there are only two options in life — and *only two results:* those who trust in horses "collapse and fall"; those who boast of the name of God "shall rise and stand upright" (v. 8).

If the couriers of your life bring you breathless news of threatened attack, in what do you boast? Education, prestige, cleverness, reputation, wealth? Like horses and chariots, they cannot stand.

Let your boasting, your hoping, your glorying be in the name of the Lord God of Israel and of his Son, Jesus Christ. Such boasting is never bad.

Prayer: *Holy Father, lead us in the celebration of your name. Let the banners of our praise be lifted to the winds of life. Let them shout as they wave that you are the God of victory, and that our boasting – all our boasting – is only in you. Through Christ your conquering Son, we pray. Amen.*

CHAPTER 10

How to Praise God
in the Midst of Suffering

Psalm 22

Let me tell you about three of my friends, three friends who taught me lessons about suffering. Then I'll tell you about a fourth friend. "Friend" I call him, though I've never met him. But he too has taught me a great deal about suffering. Three friends, then a fourth, and finally a fifth, who knows more than anyone else about suffering.

If I use the stories of my friends to talk about suffering and how we can praise God in the midst of it, it is because suffering is always personal. It is *people* who suffer. Suffering is not an abstract idea but a real experience, not an academic theory but a trying episode in life.

The first of my friends is Marilyn. Some months ago her apartment house caught fire and she lost every material thing she owned. On her school teacher's salary she had to pick up the pieces of her life and set up housekeeping again. I saw her just a few weeks after this happened and was encouraged by her outlook. No bitterness, no anxiety, no despair. Little by little she was trying to replace what she had lost and praising God along the way. The experience had been painful but not devastating. She may have been puzzled by questions; she was not rocked by doubt. God went with her through the suffering, and his presence kept her steady.

The second of my friends is Dick. As head of a manufacturing company, he went through a nerve-wracking experience — a massive fire that wiped out his plant, his inventory, and his equipment — nearly four million dollars in damage. His production schedules were thrown off, his growth projections were set back at least a year. We talked about this while he was still digging his way out of the rubble.

"People sometimes think that spiritual growth comes from mountain-top experiences," he reminded me. "But that's not true in my experience," he went on to say. "Any spiritual growth I've ever made has taken place in the valley. In fact I can say that I have learned most and grown fastest when God has allowed me to be clobbered." Amid the ashes that burned his business and charred his financial hopes, he was praising God. He did not enjoy the experience, but he did grow through it. And that's more important.

The third of my friends is a woman whose name I can't remember. She came up to me after a service when I had been preaching about joy in the midst of suffering. She wore a patch over one eye, and her face was marked with the scars of surgery. Her story brought tears to my eyes. She had cancer in many parts of her body. She had been through at least a half-dozen major operations. "You were right," she said, "when you told the people that God can give joy even when we suffer. Many nights I've walked the hospital floor waiting for the pain shots to take hold so I could sleep, and I've rejoiced that God is with me." "You should have preached the sermon," I told her. "You know far more about suffering than I do."

Three friends whom God asked to walk a painful road and who knew that he was with them in their pain — they taught me more than they know, and I pass their lessons on to you.

The fourth friend of mine lived nearly three thousand years ago. In a sense, his experience is basic to that of my other three friends. He was one of the first men of faith to record in detail his suffering and to recount his praise of God in the midst of it. Psalm 22 is what we call the account of what he went through. It has been a pattern for sufferers to follow ever since, a psalm for all seasons, especially seasons of suffering.

If our psalmist were to summarize the advice that his suffering equipped him to give us, here is what he would say: first, keep in touch with God; next, believe that God has some purpose in your suffering; then, ask him for deliverance; finally, rejoice in his victory ahead of time. Let's hear how this advice was hammered out on the anvil of his own anguish.

Keep in Touch with God

Suffering at its worst is what the opening words of the psalm describe: "My God, my God, why hast thou forsaken me? Why art thou so far from helping me, from the words of my groaning? O my God, I cry by day, but thou dost not answer; and by night, but find no rest" (vv. 1-2).

The sufferer feels abandoned, not just by friends or family but by the One on whom his very life depends — his God, his Lord. The One who promised never to leave or forsake his own has seemingly vanished from the scene. The Father of

Israel, who urges his children to call upon him in time of need, has apparently turned deaf to the plea of his loved one. This is suffering at its sharpest.

But the sufferer refuses to settle for absolute despair. He does not sink into the silence of utter depression. He is depressed, but not so deeply that he cannot speak, and he cries out to God. He keeps in touch with him despite his pain and anxiety.

His enemies savagely seek his hurt: "Many bulls encompass me, strong bulls of Bashan surround me; they open wide their mouths at me, like a ravening and roaring lion. . . . Yea, dogs are round about me; a company of evildoers encircle me; they have pierced my hands and feet — I can count all my bones — they stare and gloat over me; they divide my garments among them, and for my raiment they cast lots" (vv. 12-13, 16-18).

Heedless of his pain, greedy for his good, his enemies wait to take advantage of his misfortune. And he barely has strength to hang on: "I am poured out like water, and all my bones are out of joint; my heart is like wax, it is melted within my breast; my strength is dried up like a potsherd, and my tongue cleaves to my jaws; thou dost lay me in the dust of death" (vv. 14-15).

Harassed by his enemies and hurting inside, this fourth friend of ours keeps in touch with God. Though he *feels* abandoned by God, he *knows* better. And honestly, passionately, thoroughly, he brings his problems to God's attention.

Believe That God Has Some Purpose in It

Suffering shakes and stuns us. In our state of shock we are apt to brand the whole experience senseless. But the psalmist refuses to do this. By bringing his problem to God, by remembering God's past help, by expecting God's rescue, our friend is really acknowledging that God may have some purpose in his pain.

Not that he says so explicitly, but he leaves room for us to read between the lines. If we are not able to find some sense in suffering, the alternatives are pretty frightful. We can call it an accident, something that happened for no reason at all. But when we do, we are really saying that life is out of control, that God cannot always care for his people. This is a scary point of view. How can we trust a God who loses his grip just when we need him to hold tightly to us?

Or we can blame our suffering on the devil and his troops, demons we call them. Again, this is a fearful option. If the devil can make us suffer in ways that God does not approve, then isn't the devil stronger than God? Doesn't this mean that evil is running the universe?

Even when his enemies are tightening the screws and stretching the rack, the psalmist knows that he is really in God's hands, as he always has been. "Yet thou art he who took me from the womb; thou didst keep me safe upon my mother's breasts. Upon thee was I cast from my birth, and since my mother bore me thou hast been my God. Be not far from me, for trouble is near and there is none to help" (vv. 9-11).

Believe that God has some purpose in your suffering, and as you do you will be able to accept your difficulties and not be destroyed by them. Not that we can immediately discover what that purpose is. God does not always tell. Like Job, we are called to maintain our faith while kept in ignorance. We can do this as we remember all that God has been to us in the past. His unchanging love gives us courage to face present hardships and to fit them into his good purposes for us.

Ask God for Deliverance

All this talk of finding purpose in suffering does not mean that we relish it or that we go around looking for it. It still hurts, and we seek relief from it. By his example, the psalmist advises us to ask God for deliverance. "But thou, O Lord, be not far off! O thou my help, hasten to my aid! Deliver my soul from the sword, my life from the power of the dog! Save me from the mouth of the lion, my afflicted soul from the horns of the wild oxen!" (vv. 19-21).

This blunt, direct plea for help is based on what God has done before: "In thee our fathers trusted; they trusted, and thou didst deliver them. To thee they cried, and were saved; in thee they trusted, and were not disappointed" (vv. 4-5).

God's past record gives us hope in our wretched present. Our confidence now is grounded on what he did then. And we can ask him to come to our aid. Savior is one of his great names.

Rejoice in God's Victory Ahead of Time

The psalmist's last word of advice is based on the first three. Keep in touch with God, he has told us. Believe that he has some purpose in our suffering. Then, ask him for deliverance. After that, take one further step: rejoice in God's victory ahead of time. Here's the way the psalmist does this: "I will tell of thy name to my brethren; in the midst of the congregation I will praise thee: You who fear the Lord, praise him! all you sons of Jacob, glorify him, and stand in awe of him, all you sons of Israel! For he has not despised or abhorred the affliction of the afflicted; and he has not hid his face from him, but has heard, when he cried to him" (vv. 22-24).

Trust at its best, this is. In the midst of his anguish the sufferer looks forward and upward. He knows who God is, what he is like, what he can do. And he not only praises God but invites his friends to join the celebration.

Four friends who trusted God and honored his name in the furnace of suffering — a school teacher whose goods were destroyed, a business man whose factory was burned, a woman riddled by cancer, a psalmist oppressed by his enemies. But the fifth Friend is the greatest of all. In a garden he sweat drops of blood, yet he kept in touch with God and believed in God's purposes. On a cross he asked for deliverance and thanked God for victory ahead of time. His words from the cross are significant. In the midst of them he echoed our psalmist's cry, "My God, my God, why hast thou forsaken me?" He ended by commending his spirit to his Father. And along the way he prayed for his enemies, forgave a thief, and cared for his mother. Jesus Christ served God in the midst of suffering. In so doing he leaves us more than an example. He gives us grace and power to do the same.

Prayer: *Father, teach us to sing another form of doxology. Not only "praise God from whom all blessings flow" but "praise God when any suffering comes." Thank you, Father, for friends who have taught us lessons and particularly for the great Friend, Jesus Christ, who endured shame because of the joy of carrying out your purposes. Help us to keep learning from him. We pray in his name. Amen.*

CHAPTER 11

Who Really Owns
Your Property?

Psalm 24

The land in Southern California originally belonged to the king of Spain. At least that is what
is stated in the title report that traces the ownership of our property back to the days of the
California missions. When the courageous padres
like Father Serra and Father Lasuen founded those
twenty-one missions a day's journey apart on El
Camino Real, the royal highway, which stretched
from San Diego to north of San Francisco, they
claimed the surrounding land for the Spanish
Crown.

When the Mexican people gained their inde-
pendence from Spain, they secularized the missions
in the 1830's and turned their lands into ranches
that grazed thousands of sheep and cattle. The
period of the Mexican ranches was cut short by the
invasion of General Fremont and his army, who
claimed California for the United States. After
statehood in 1850, the great ranches were even-
tually divided into smaller farms and the tiny towns
began to swell with settlers who heard that the hills
were paved with gold.

As the towns elbowed their way into the country-
side, the subdividers began to transform the orange
groves and avocado orchards into villages where

each house looked like the other houses. California suburban life had begun.

Yet the houses were not really the same, because each belonged to a different owner. And each owner had proof — in the form of a title policy — that he or she was the rightful owner of the property. Title companies guarantee ownership by tracing the various transactions through which the property has been passed from hand to hand: the present owner bought it from a land developer, who in turn bought it from a farmer whose great grandfather had bought it from a Mexican ranchero, who had bought it from the Mexican government, which had won it from the king of Spain.

The rights of ownership have a long and noble history. They are protected in the Bill of Rights of the United States Constitution, which guards our properties against unreasonable searches and seizures. This protection has roots that go back through Anglo-Saxon common law to the good soil of the Old Testament. What are the commandments against stealing and coveting but divinely ordained rules to safeguard property?

Boundary lines, deeds, laws against harsh foreclosure, provisions for settling disputes over ownership, the right of an owner to pass his property on to his heirs — all of these rights that are fundamental to our society have a biblical basis. Queen Jezebel learned at great cost the dangers of tampering with these rights when she commandeered the vineyard that belonged to Naboth and paid with her life for her greed (I Kings 21; II Kings 9).

Titles to property are important. But they are also incomplete. In Southern California, the search for ownership usually ends with the king of Spain.

It should really go back two other steps: to the Indians who roamed the land before 1769 when Serra landed in San Diego, and to God who made and owns the land.

God's Ownership of All Creation

Human rights to ownership are important — but not ultimate. The Bible guards them, but it does not deify them. The prophets and the apostles recognized the title beyond the titles, the Owner above all owners.

They took their cue from the psalmists who celebrated God's ownership of all creation: "The earth is the Lord's and the fulness thereof, the world and those who dwell therein" (v. 1). *A comprehensive statement* this is. To the *Lord* (the Hebrew word order names him first) belongs the world with all its goods and people. No thing, no place, no body is exempt from his claim. There is no partnership; there are no stockholders. God is the sole, the exclusive, the total owner of all of reality.

A bold affirmation this is. The claims of rival gods are brushed aside. Dagon of the Philistines is not master of the great coastal plain. Yahweh, Lord of Israel, is. Chemosh, god of the Moabites, is not ruler of the highlands east of the Dead Sea. Yahweh, God of the tribes of Jacob, is. Marduk is not king of the Tigris-Euphrates valley. Yahweh, King of the covenant with Abraham, is.

The nations of the world may shape their conquests and remake their maps, but the earth still belongs to the Lord. The captains of industry may cut their timber, pump their oil, refine their ore, but the earth still belongs to the Lord.

You and I may save our money, hoard our down payment, pay off our mortgage, keep our taxes

85

current, but the earth — including those bits of it that we claim — still belongs to the Lord.

A reasonable assumption this is. To the Lord belongs the world with all its goods and people, and the reason for this is clear — he alone is the Creator: "for he has founded it upon the seas, and established it upon the rivers" (v. 2). Not a squatter on the property of others, not a rustler of the goods of others, God owns the world because *he* made it, not someone else.

The worshipers who sang this psalm in the Temple were reminded of the supremacy of their Lord every time they sang the phrases "upon the seas" and "upon the rivers." Both *sea* and *river* were revered as deities by their Canaanite neighbors. But the Israelites knew better. They knew that the sea and the river were merely part of the building materials with which God had carried out his creative work.

As we sing this old psalm we can find in it a similar reminder. Our neighbors can speak with awe about the wonders of "mother nature"; they can cite with curiosity the mysteries of evolution; they can salute with pride the achievements of our scientists. But we know better. We know that behind all such wonders, mysteries, and achievements lies the presence of the Creator — the Builder and Owner of all creation.

I blinked in dismay as I watched two teen-aged girls leave the auditorium of the United States Congress on Evangelism some years ago. The blonde was smoking a corncob pipe; the brunette was boasting a badge that called "CREATE." I mused on the scene as I strolled back to my hotel. Though I did not relish the sight of a girl smoking a pipe, it was the message carried by the other girl that troubled me more deeply. "CREATE" her badge shouted, as though people really could do that. It was an insolent slogan, an idolatrous motto, a symbol of much that is wrong with us. It tries to bridge the gulf between people and God. But it is a bridge that will not reach. Try as we will, *we* cannot found the earth upon the sea or establish it upon the rivers. Only *God* can do that.

Our Response to God's Ownership

What we *can* do is to respond to God's ownership. The psalmist showed us how. The strong statements about God's ownership and his creative power are followed by a question — a question that shows how impressed, how awed, we should be when we consider God's greatness: "Who shall ascend the hill of the Lord? And who shall stand in his holy place?" (v. 3). If God is this great, the question asks, if he is this powerful, if he is the owner of all of us and all our goods, who of us would dare approach him? Who of us would be allowed to come before his presence? What is our proper response to God's ownership of the universe, including us?

The pilgrims who asked these questions as they approached the gates of the Jerusalem Temple were on the right track. The very fact that they took God's greatness so seriously showed that they knew what part of their response must be — *worship*.

God was not their pal, their buddy, their crony. He was their Owner and Maker. They had to meet his demands; he did not have to meet theirs. And the first of his demands was their worship: their declaration of dependence on him, their affirmation of allegiance to him, their confession of devotion to him, their pledge of love for him,

Obedience as well as worship was to be their response. As Owner and Maker he sets the standards of our lives. The answer given by the priests to the pilgrims shows what these standards are. The pilgrims asked what qualifications a worshiper needed to stand in God's presence. The priests' answer centered in loyal obedience: "He who has clean hands and a pure heart, who does not lift up his soul to what is false, and does not swear deceitfully" (v. 4). This is a marvelous summary of godly loyalty. "Clean hands" means freedom from violence, from harsh or cruel dealings with others. "A pure heart" points to the importance of our motivation. *Heart,* in biblical language, is the place where we do our choosing. It speaks of the singleness of our devotion to God's will. We not only do what he wants, but we *want* to do what he wants. Lifting up the soul to "what is false" is a clear reference to idolatry. The Creator-Owner has no tolerance of rivals. Our false gods are not in his class, and he urges us to set them aside as a mark of our loyal obedience to him.

Worship, obedience, and *delight* are the ingredients in our response. God not only demands our exclusive allegiance; he promises exquisite blessings: "He will receive blessing from the Lord, and vindication from the God of his salvation" (v. 5). Our loyalty to God is more than matched by his loyalty to us. He will do all that his relationship to us requires. Protection, provision, forgiveness, power — these are just a few of the blessings that the ancient priests promised to those who cast their lot with the Lord.

Our delight in God is not only based on what he will do but on who he is. The final verses of our psalm ring with this kind of delight. The pilgrims, eager for worship, called for the Temple gates to be opened and for God to flood the Temple with his presence: "Lift up your heads, O gates! and be lifted up, O ancient doors! that the King of glory may come in" (v. 7). The priests within the Temple tested again the loyalty of the pilgrims by making sure that they knew who the true God is: "Who is the King of glory?" (v. 8). The final answer of the pilgrims was the signal for the gates to open. It was an answer that summed up the power and glory of the Lord who made and owns the world including us and our property: "The Lord of hosts, he is the King of glory!" (v. 10). The Lord of the armies of heaven and earth, the Lord who has the stars, the angels, and the nations at his beck and call — he is the glorious King, our King. We can delight in his ownership; we can delight in him.

This psalm is much more than a liturgy sung by priests and pilgrims. It is a song of life, a life-giving song. It tells us what our Owner is like, and what he asks of us. It reminds us that the title to our property goes back not just to the king of Spain but to the King of glory. And it reminds us that the title to our hands, our hearts, our souls goes back to him as well.

Prayer: *Our Father, we thank you for these basic lessons about who we are, where we came from, and to whom we belong. In our living and in our giving, in our saving and in our sharing, lead us to put these lessons to work in the world that you made and that you own. Through Jesus Christ, your Son and our Lord. Amen.*

CHAPTER 12

How to Listen to the Thunder

Psalm 29

Thunder rocked the house until the eaves creaked and the windows rattled. I stooped down to look under the bed and found myself face to face with two dark, shiny eyes — and a wet nose. Our dog Pepi was trembling in terror as I fished him out of his hiding place. Fortunately, thunder is an experience less frequent in Southern California than in some other parts of the world. Were it not, Pepi would have been a nervous wreck long ago. His problem is simple: he does not know how to listen to the thunder.

And he is not alone. I have seen grown men and women blanch with fear as the thunder rolled its way through the lowering skies. In the days before jet airplanes could soar above the storms, the propeller-driven planes would have to fly around the storms or through them. I have felt a plane jump and jerk and watched the lightning set the surrounding sky on fire. I have seen fellow passengers bite their lips and squeeze the arm rests until their knuckles turned white.

Thunderstorms can be an awesome experience. Sometimes they sound like a chorus of massive tympani drums as their roll shakes the land from horizon to horizon. At other times the thunder rings out in a sharp crack like the snap of a giant bullwhip.

To our puppy, thunder is an unpleasant sound whose origin he does not understand or care to understand. To many people, thunder is a natural phenomenon usually accompanied by lightning and heavy rain. Its deeper message they do not hear.

In contrast, the men and women of Israel as they gathered for worship celebrated thunder as the voice of God: "The voice of the Lord is upon the waters; the God of glory thunders, the Lord, upon many waters. The voice of the Lord is powerful, the voice of the Lord is full of majesty" (vv. 3-4). They believed not so much in *nature* as in *creation*. They saw their whole environment as derived from God, as dependent on God, as sustained and renewed by God. They interpreted their surroundings not in terms of natural laws, which mechanically programmed the movement of the stars and the turning of the seasons, but in terms of the hand of God who personally directed the course of events in ways that declared his majesty. What these men and women of faith saw around them was alive with the glory of God; what they heard in the sounds of the universe — especially in the thunder — was the voice of the Lord.

Their perspective on the world must not go out of season. When it comes to understanding the deepest secrets of the universe, their faith will give us more help than our science — as helpful as our science has been.

Were we to have caught them fresh from their worship and sought their advice on how we too might listen to the thunder, they would have responded with at least two words of exhortation: revere the God of the creation and remember the God of the covenant. These are the exhortations that ring through the verses of Psalm 29.

Revere the God of the Creation
The first words of the psalm reach to the very heights of heaven and remind us of the lofty enterprise of which we are a part as we worship: "Ascribe

to the Lord, O heavenly beings, ascribe to the Lord glory and strength. Ascribe to the Lord the glory of his name; worship the Lord in holy array" (vv. 1-2). The angels are urged to lead the worship. God's magnificence — his glory and strength — are to be celebrated in heaven as well as on earth. In fact, the heavenly beings (literally the *sons of God,* a term frequently used for angels in the Old Testament) are the leaders of the chorus.

The singers of this psalm sensed that *they were not alone in their worship.* There is a whole other world as real as the one we live in — perhaps more real — that lives to praise the Most High God. The Old Testament people of God only rarely saw angels, only infrequently heard their voices. But they knew them to be part of reality. And they knew that the angelic mission was like the human mission: it centered in the praise of God.

Isaiah's vision made this clear: "In the year that King Uzziah died I saw the Lord sitting upon a throne, high and lifted up; and his train filled the temple. Above him stood the seraphim. . . . And one called to another and said: 'Holy, holy, holy is the Lord of hosts; the whole earth is full of his glory' " (Isaiah 6:1-3). Inexpressibly holy, too holy for words — that was the seraphim's evaluation of God. As part of the great creation, angels make the celebration of God's uniqueness and God's worthiness the theme of their songs.

The singers of this psalm sensed that *they needed help in their worship.* The best of the Israelites knew that their thoughts were not lofty enough to embrace the ways of God; they knew that their words were not exalted enough to describe the works of God. They called upon the *angels* to help.

And angels have a way with words. One of their tasks in history has been to make the great announcements. To the old priest Zechariah, an angel appeared with words like these: "Do not be afraid, Zechariah, for your prayer is heard, and your wife Elizabeth will bear you a son, and you shall call his name John" (Luke 1:13). To a peasant girl in Nazareth, an angel brought this news: "And behold, you will conceive in your womb and bear a son, and you shall call his name Jesus" (Luke 1:31).

Angels have a way with words, and they have an intimate knowledge of God. After all, they stand before the throne of God and behold his face. Unhampered by sin, unmarred by the fall, untouched by the curse, angels perceive God through undimmed eyes and unaddled minds. Small wonder, then, that the singers of the psalm began their burst of praise with a call to the angels to lead the anthem that would salute the glory and strength of God.

The universe that is geared to praise God not only includes the angels, it counts the *thunder* and *lightning* as key voices in its chorus: "The voice of the Lord is upon the waters; the God of glory thunders, the Lord, upon many waters" (v. 3). The picture here may be of a storm at sea — like the one on the Mediterranean that nearly swamped Jonah's ship, or the one on Galilee that panicked Jesus' disciples. More likely, the waters mentioned are those depicted in the story of creation in Genesis: "And God said, 'Let there be a firmament in the midst of the waters, and let it separate the waters from the waters.' And God made the firmament and separated the waters which were under the firmament from the waters which were above the firmament. And it was so. And God called the firmament Heaven . . ." (Genesis 1:6-8).

". . . the waters which were above the firmament" were close to the throne of God which was "over the flood" (v. 10). In the thunder, then, the worshipers in Israel heard the voice of God sounding from his throne and echoing across the heavenly waters. The heavy rain that accompanied the thunder they would have understood as the release of some of those heavenly waters.

The volume of the thunder and the force of the storm were heard and seen as signs of the majesty, the lordliness, of their God. An *impressive majesty* they found it. Not even strong trees and high mountains can stand before it: "The voice of the Lord breaks the cedars, the Lord breaks the cedars of Lebanon. He makes Lebanon to skip like a calf, and Sirion like a young wild ox" (vv. 5-6). The stately cedars on the massive mountains of Lebanon were often a symbol of strength and stability to the people of the Old Testament. So was the range of hills around Mt. Hermon, here called Sirion. Yet God's power was impressive enough to set the mountains dancing.

An *inescapable majesty* they saw it to be. Not only the mountains to the north, but the deserts to the south are seared and rocked when God's lightning races and God's thunder rolls: "The voice of the Lord flashes forth flames of fire. The voice of the Lord shakes the wilderness, the Lord shakes the wilderness of Kadesh" (vv. 7-8). As God had shaken the desert in the days of Moses, when the law thundered from Sinai, so his inescapable presence was still felt by the pilgrims who gathered for worship.

Revere the God of the creation, the psalmist shouts down the generations to us. The Lord of angels, of cedars and oaks, of hills and deserts, is worthy of worship. In revering this God we learn how to listen to the thunder.

Remember the God of the Covenant

Astounded at the glory of God, these worshipers

94

contemplated the thunder and lightning. But they did so not as spectators but as participants. The God of the creation was also the God of the covenant. His grand design included them.

An *eternal majesty* they acknowledged in their God: "The Lord sits enthroned over the flood; the Lord sits enthroned as king for ever" (v. 10). No heir apparent was ready to ascend his throne; no usurper could topple him by revolution. His kingship was eternal.

Yet he was open to the needs of his people. His was an *effective majesty,* responsive to the needs of those to whom he had linked himself in covenant. No wild force of nature was he, no blind principle of fertility, no mindless planet spinning a relentless course through the cosmos. He who thundered till the mountains reeled, sat hushed to hear the prayers of his people: "May the Lord give strength to his people! May the Lord bless his people with peace!" (v. 11). Strength and peace — power to cope with all difficulties, well-being in the midst of struggles — these are the twin gifts of the mighty God. His *ability* to respond is manifested in the creation; his *willingness* to respond is demonstrated in the covenant.

What do you do when the thunder rolls? You can run and hide like our timid pup; you can blame the weatherman like most of your neighbors.

Or you can revere the majestic Lord of all weather and rejoice that through his lordly Son he has offered strength and peace to the dwellers of our fragile planet. When you do that, you will have learned to listen to the thunder.

Prayer: *Majestic Lord, glorious King, loving Savior, help us to hear your voice both in the sounds of storm and in the gentle call of your divine Son, Jesus Christ, through whom we pray. Amen.*

Conclusion

These twelve psalms are not antiques to be dusted and polished. The are living expressions of trust and worship.

And they are not just artifacts to be studied. They are hymns and prayers to be sung in the high and low moments of life.

Nor are they mere masterpieces of art to be admired. They are ringing testimonies to faith, vital witnesses to hope, fervent invitations to love.

They are life-changing, like the experience of finding a friend whose warmth and compassion make things new. They are life-preserving, like the taking of a tonic whose powers invigorate the body and refresh the spirit. They are life-directing, like the discovery of a map in a time of anxious, aimless wandering.

It is the power of the Psalms that one verse or one stanza can change life's direction, heal life's hurts, or chart life's course. I trust that this power has touched your thinking, eased your pain, and stirred your devotion. The Lord of the psalmists is yet at work among his creatures. Because he has not changed, his psalms are always in season.